INDIAN COOKBOOK

2 Books in 1: A 140 Recipes Journey For Traditional Dishes From India

Maki Blanc
Emma Yang

INDIAN
COOKBOOK

70 Easy Recipes For Naan Tandoori Chicken And Traditional Dishes From India

---

Emma Yang

© Copyright 2021 by Emma Yang - All rights reserved.

This document is geared towards providing exact and reliable information in regard to the topic and issue covered. The publication is sold with the idea that the publisher is not required to render accounting, officially permitted, or otherwise, qualified services. If advice is necessary, legal or professional, a practiced individual in the profession should be ordered.

From a Declaration of Principles which was accepted and approved equally by a Committee of the American Bar Association and a Committee of Publishers and Associations.

In no way is it legal to reproduce, duplicate, or transmit any part of this document in either electronic means or in printed format. Recording of this publication is strictly prohibited and any storage of this document is not allowed unless with written permission from the publisher. All rights reserved.

The information provided herein is stated to be truthful and consistent, in that any liability, in terms of inattention or otherwise, by any usage or abuse of any policies, processes, or directions contained within is the solitary and utter responsibility of the recipient reader. Under no circumstances will any legal responsibility or blame be held against the publisher for any reparation, damages, or monetary loss due to the information herein, either directly or indirectly.

Respective authors own all copyrights not held by the publisher.

The information herein is offered for informational purposes solely and is universal as so. The presentation of the information is without contract or any type of guarantee assurance.

The trademarks that are used are without any consent, and the publication of the trademark is without permission or backing by the trademark owner. All trademarks and brands within this book are for clarifying purposes only and are owned by the owners themselves, not affiliated with this document.

Contents

INTRODUCTION 11

CHAPTER 1: INTRODUCTION TO INDIAN FOOD 12

1.1 History and Origin of Indian Food 12

1.2 History of Traditional Food 14

1.3 Indian Food According to Nutrition and Dietetics 16

1.4 Various Ingredients Used in Indian Food 16

1.5 Evolution of Indian Food Over Time 18

CHAPTER 2: THE WORLD OF INDIAN BREAKFAST RECIPES 19

2.1 Indian Aloo Paratha Recipe 19

2.2 Indian Dosa Recipe 20

2.3 Indian Appam Recipe 21

2.4 Indian Namkeen Seviyan Recipe 23

2.5 Indian Spiced Omelet Recipe 24

2.6 Indian Poha Recipe 25

2.7 Indian Aloo Puri Recipe 26

2.8 Indian Scrambled Eggs Recipe 27

2.9 Indian Oats Kheer Recipe 28

2.10 Indian Rava Idli Recipe 29

CHAPTER 3: THE WORLD OF INDIAN LUNCH RECIPES 31

3.1 Indian Curry Oatmeal with Tandoori Masala Roasted Zucchini Recipe..................31

3.2 Indian Chicken Biryani Recipes..................33

3.3 Indian Naan Pizza with Roasted Chicken Recipe..................34

3.4 Indian Capsicum Rice Recipe..................35

3.5 Indian Aval Upma Recipe..................37

3.6 Indian Style Chicken and Onions Recipe..................38

3.7 Indian Tomato Rice Recipe..................40

3.8 Indian Chicken Curry Recipe..................41

3.9 Indian Butter Chicken Recipe..................43

3.10 Indian Chili Chicken Recipe..................44

3.11 Indian Cashew Chicken Recipe..................45

3.12 Indian Paneer Burji Recipe..................47

3.13 Indian Chicken Tikka Masala Recipe..................48

3.14 Indian Cauliflower Tikka Masala Curry Recipe..................49

3.15 Indian Roasted Vegetables Recipe..................50

3.16 Indian Moong Daal Kichri Recipe..................52

3.17 Indian Rajma Chawal Recipe..................54

3.18 Indian Mattar Paneer Recipe..................55

3.19 Indian Paneer Tikka Masala Recipe..................57

3.20 Indian Spiced Vegetable Burger Recipe..................58

CHAPTER 4: THE WORLD OF INDIAN DINNER RECIPES 60

4.1 Indian Chicken Qorma Recipe 60

4.2 Indian Dum Aloo Recipe 61

4.3 Indian Palak Paneer Recipe 63

4.4 Indian Tamarind Rice Recipe 64

4.5 Indian Samber Recipe 65

4.6 Indian Daal Fry Recipe 66

4.7 Indian Parippu Curry Recipe 68

4.8 Indian Style Fried Fish Recipe 69

4.9 Indian Kerela Barta Recipe 70

4.10 Indian Kofta Recipe 71

4.11 Indian Missi Roti Recipe 72

4.12 Indian Murgh Mussalam Recipe 74

4.13 Indian Rongi Recipe 75

4.14 Indian Shahi Paneer Recipe 77

4.15 Indian Chetinadu Chicken Recipe 78

4.16 Indian Fried Kerala and Beef Recipe 79

4.17 Indian Sevai Recipe 82

4.18 Indian Stuffed Mushroom Recipe 83

4.19 Indian Grilled Fish Recipe 84

4.20 Indian Mixed Vegetables Recipe 86

CHAPTER 5: THE WORLD OF INDIAN DESSERT RECIPES 88

5.1 Indian Bread Malpua Recipe 88

5.2 Indian Gulab Jamun Recipe 89

5.3 Indian Instant Pot Coconut Rice Kheer Recipe 90

5.4 Indian Bread Pudding Recipe 92

5.5 Indian Carrot Halwa Recipe 93

5.6 Indian Rava Kessari Recipe 95

5.7 Indian Coconut Laddu Recipe 96

5.8 Indian Basundi Recipe 97

5.9 Indian Mango Shirkhand Recipe 98

5.10 Indian Moong Daal Halwa Recipe 99

CHAPTER 6: AUTHENTIC INDIAN RECIPES EATEN ONLY BY INDIAN PEOPLE 100

6.1 Indian Vada Pav Recipe 100

6.2 Indian Dhokla Recipe 102

6.3 Indian Masala Dosa Recipe 103

6.4 Indian Babinka Recipe 104

6.5 Indian Bamboo Steam Fish Recipe 105

6.6 Indian Kondi Kura Recipe 105

6.7 Indian Bhuttay ke Kheer Recipe 106

6.8 Indian Sidu Recipe 107

6.9 Indian Tabak Maax Recipe 108

6.10 Indian Sarson ka Saag Recipe..109

CONCLUSION...111

Introduction

For quite a long time, different countries of the world have idealized their expertise with flavors to change the boring materials to tasteful ones. Indian cuisine is not the cooking of only a single ethnicity. However, the roots of this cooking style go back hundreds of years and is a blend of the cooking of numerous identities and societies such as Greece, Phoenicians, Chinese, Muslims, Portuguese, and different Europeans. It has been affected extensively by climatic conditions, customs, tastes, health, and religions, specifically Hinduism and Islam.

They think about food and drink to support the soul just as the body. Food in India is essential to otherworldly progression too. It is a source of delight and festivity. The Indian kitchen differs essentially from south to north and east to west. The southern and western Indian cooking styles drive the method of veggie lover Indian food, as most Westerners have come to know and adore it.

You can prepare Indian dishes at home by learning various ingredients that you will need to start cooking. By reading this wonderful book, you will get detailed knowledge regarding the nutritional value and history of traditional Indian dishes. This book contains over 70 different breakfast, lunch, dinner, dessert, and dishes eaten only by Indian people. You can easily start cooking at home with the detailed instructions present below each recipe. So start reading and start cooking today!

Chapter 1: Introduction to Indian Food

Indians view their food as an important part of their lives. Cooking is viewed as craftsmanship, and moms start to show their girls and pass down family plans to them for the most part. Eating times are significant events for the family to get together. Most suppers contain a few dishes going from staples like rice and pieces of bread to meat and vegetables and a flavorful dessert at the end of every meal.

In most of Indian homes, food varieties are produced from scratch by using new fixings. For example, a few families purchase their wheat, wash it, dry it in the sun, and bring it into a flour factory to have it ground into flour precisely in the manner they like, instead of purchasing the already prepared flour from a store. This is changing in greater urban areas where individuals have progressively busy lives, and they are glad to utilize pre-made ingredients.

1.1 History and Origin of Indian Food

India is a land that is enriched with culture and immense legacy. This is reflected in the variety of food that has arisen throughout the country through the ages. It is protected to say that the Indian cuisine is by a wide margin the most assorted one in its taste and the utilization of differed fixings. Indian food is celebrated all around for the utilization of flavors like saffron, coriander, ginger, cumin, cloves, and a few others that improve the desire for each dish. An assortment of spices and privately discovered components have integrated various types of procedures that can be found as an internationally famous cooking today.

The history of Indian cuisine traces back to over 10000 years and has been exceptionally affected by Hindu and Muslim customs. The principal features that we consider in Indian cooking are flavors, fiery tastes, and vegetables. Truly it is the biggest trademark, continually considering the hugeness of this country and the number of various styles as per the districts. A few groups feel that the smell of flavors was what pulled in the British to India.

The patterns from different countries have been blended and intertwined with those of India. It has brought about the cooking that we know today, with that aggregate of flavors, surfaces, and structures as different as its kin and culture.

The historical backdrop of Indian food runs directly back from the Harappan times. In this period, wheat, rice, millet, chickpeas, and lentils shaped the staples of the normal Indian diet. A few citruses and different natural products were utilized to add flavor. The well-known utilization of cinnamon can likewise be traced all the way back to these occasions. The grains were made into stews or soups in which cinnamon was utilized. At last, grain began being heated into level pieces of bread which are today prominently known as chapatis or naan.

Accordingly, the root of Indian cooking can be traced back hundreds of years earlier. These various areas had their nearby components to assemble surprisingly delightful dinners that are appreciated even today. These are pervasive in Indian homes as well as delighted worldwide, where a profound appreciation for the Indian flavors can be seen. The variety and flavor of Indian food have advanced through the ages. Hence, these delightful Hindu dishes are adding shading and flavor to lives all throughout the planet.

1.2 History of Traditional Food

The history of traditional foods goes way back in medieval time. The word 'biryani' starts from the Persian word 'birian', which signifies 'fried prior to cooking'. Rumors say that Mumtaz Mahal, Shah Jahan's sovereign, when visited the armed force military enclosure, thought that the warriors were injured. Accordingly, she requested that the culinary expert set up an exceptional dish, which gave adjusted nourishment. After a couple of dismissals, she finally chose biryani, considering it the total supper which could be eaten as a single serving. So while the main inceptions of this dish have Persian and Afghani impacts, the Mughals created it inside the tremendous Indian subcontinent they controlled for quite a long time.

The story of Idli happens in the Kannada composing 'Vaddaradhane' in 970 A.D., where it highlights as one of the eighteen things served to a Brahmachari who visits the home of a woman. However, the three components of present-day Idli production are the utilization of rice corn meal alongside urad dal, the long maturation of the blend, and steaming the batter to featheriness.

Paneer is a fundamental ingredient in most Indian dishes, Palak Paneer being the most celebrated of all, particularly in the umpteen veggie-lover families that spot the country. Hardly any individuals realize that paneer, supposedly, was really an incidental development. As the hypothesis goes, the Mongols were out on a long excursion, riding ponies that were giving milk in Mushkis (packs made of crude cover-up). The warmth of deserts and the rennet in the calfskin transformed the milk into paneer.

They tasted the resultant item and discovered it to be somewhat tasty. It was brought to India a long time ago by the Mughals and was blended in with different Indian flavors and vegetables, which at last turned into a staple that we would all be able to confirm today.

Pav Bhaji is a dish that supposedly started in the city of Mumbai. Consistently, various laborers would eat it in breaks that were excessively short for a full feast. As they needed to get back to their work soon, a light lunch was preferred to a substantial one. Seeing the situation of the laborers, a nearby merchant made the dish utilizing extra elements of different dishes accessible on the menu. Roti or rice, which would be put aside for different dishes, was supplanted with pav bhaji. The flavors of many traditional dishes remain the same even today.

1.3 Indian Food According to Nutrition and Dietetics

Indian food is generally famous for its variety. The assortment of food sources, flavors, and dishes local to India makes Indian food quite possibly the healthiest food varieties on the planet. Nonetheless, traditional Indian food is not just fulfilling, but at the same time, it is amazingly scrumptious with plenty of health advantages. Indian food resolves insusceptibility, inflammation, mental problems, and many different issues in the human body.

An assortment of food varieties and supplements is required for trillions of cells in the human body. Indian food incorporates an assortment of flavors, where each zest has numerous health advantages. Counting an assortment of flavors and vegetables in your eating routine is significant for living a healthy life.

Pickles are made with the special type of salt (rock salt) and oil, a standout amongst other probiotic food sources that you can have. The traditional Indian chutney is made with ground salad greens and seeds.

The thought here is to tell that Indian food has consistently been supportive, healthy and fulfilling. Cook your food with healthy and customary fixings, and there is most likely no food as sound and healthy as Indian food.

1.4 Various Ingredients Used in Indian Food

There are so many ingredients used in Indian cooking. Following are a list of few ingredients that are compulsory in each dish:

1. Cloves
2. Garam masala
3. Turmeric powder
4. Chili powder
5. Cumin powder
6. Roasted cumin seeds
7. Roasted mustard seeds
8. Curry leaves
9. Fenugreek seeds
10. Coriander seeds
11. Cardamom powder
12. Saffron
13. Cinnamon powder
14. Coconut milk
15. Roasted red chilies
16. Rice flour
17. Wheat flour
18. Whole rice

19. Gram flour
20. Chickpeas
21. Beans
22. Sambar powder
23. Rasam powder
24. Mustard oil
25. Lentils
26. Ghee

All the ingredients listed above will be used in the recipes given in the subsequent chapter. All these ingredients have immense health benefits.

1.5 Evolution of Indian Food Over Time

The world sings praises about Indian food. However, the food of India is partitioned into four essential territorial styles of preparing and introducing food, specifically North Indian Cuisine, South Indian Cuisine, East Indian Cuisine, and West Indian Cuisine. In general, India has the biggest assortment of dishes that contains the sweet, pungent, and zesty groups and holds the crown of being the world's most enhanced cooking. However, current Indian food has gone through numerous progressions and acquaintances at the place where it is today.

Present-day Indian food conveys the heaviness of keeping up conventional patterns of the different Indian cooking styles which incorporate both the Hindu veggie diet and the Mughal meat rarities. Yet, it puts its very own bit by including unique cooking styles, which have helped create and widen the sense of taste of individuals in India, therefore, absorbing different food societies of the world under one rooftop.

Chapter 2: The World of Indian Breakfast Recipes

Breakfast is the first meal of the day, and Indians consider it very important. All the breakfast dishes mentioned below are healthy and are traditionally eaten in many districts of India:

2.1 Indian Aloo Paratha Recipe

Preparation Time: 15 minutes
Cooking Time: 15 minutes
Serving: 2

Ingredients:

- Oil, five tablespoon
- Mashed potatoes, two cups
- Flour, two cups
- Cumin seeds, one teaspoon
- Chopped ginger, half tablespoon
- Salt, to taste
- Turmeric powder, one teaspoon
- Green chutney, half cup
- Onion, one

Instructions:
1. Take a large bowl and add the flour into it.
2. Add the mashed potatoes and cumin seeds into it.
3. Add the salt, pepper, and chopped cilantro in it.
4. Add the chopped onions and turmeric powder.
5. Mix them well.
6. Add some oil to make dough of it.

7. Make round balls of the formed dough.
8. Dust the balls with wheat flour and roll them to make a round roti.
9. Cook the rolled paratha on the hot pan.
10. Drizzle the oil on top.
11. Cook the paratha well.
12. Your dish is ready to be served with green chutney.

2.2 Indian Dosa Recipe

Preparation Time: 30 minutes
Cooking Time: 10 minutes
Serving: 4

Ingredients:

- Poha, two tablespoon
- Regular rice, half cup
- Idli rice, half cup
- Salt, to taste
- Black pepper, to taste
- Urad dal, a quarter cup
- Methi seeds, one tablespoon
- Cooking oil, as required
- Water, one and a half cup

Instructions:
1. Take a large bowl.
2. Add all the dried ingredients into the bowl.
3. Add the water and make a thin batter.
4. Take a large pan.
5. Add the oil into the pan.

6. Add a ladle full of the batter onto the pan and spread it.
7. Cook the dosa from both sides.
8. Dish it out when it turns golden brown in color.
9. Your dish is ready to be served.

2.3 Indian Appam Recipe

Preparation Time: 30 minutes
Cooking Time: 10 minutes
Serving: 4

Ingredients:

- Poha, two tablespoon
- Regular rice, half cup
- Desiccated coconut, half cup
- Salt, to taste
- Yeast, half teaspoon
- Boiled rice, a quarter cup
- Sugar, one tablespoon
- Cooking oil, as required
- Water, one and a half cup

Instructions:
1. Take a large bowl.
2. Add all the dried ingredients into the bowl.
3. Add the water and make a thin batter.
4. Take a large pan.
5. Add the oil into the pan.
6. Add a ladle full of the batter onto the pan and spread it.
7. Cook the dosa from both sides.
8. Dish it out when it turns golden brown in color.

9. Your dish is ready to be served.

2.4 Indian Namkeen Seviyan Recipe

Preparation Time: 30 minutes
Cooking Time: 10 minutes
Serving: 4

Ingredients:

- Thin vermicelli, two cups
- Oil, two tablespoon
- Mustard seeds, one teaspoon
- Cumin seeds, one teaspoon
- Urad dal, one cup
- Green chilies, two
- Curry leaves, five
- Onion, one
- Beans, half cup
- Carrots chopped, half cup
- Chopped beans, half cup
- Fresh peas, half cup
- Tomato puree, half cup
- Turmeric powder, half teaspoon
- Roasted peanuts, two tablespoon
- Salt, to taste
- Black pepper, to taste
- Chopped garlic, half cup

Instructions:
1. Heat a pan and add the vermicelli in it.
2. Roast it for three to four minutes.
3. Heat the oil in another pan.
4. Add the urad dal, mustard and cumin seeds.
5. Add the chilies and curry leaves, beans, carrots and peanuts in it.

6. Add the salt and black pepper as required.
7. Add the turmeric powder and onions in it.
8. Add the tomatoes and water in a pan.
9. Boil the mixture well.
10. Add the roasted vermicelli and cook for five minutes.
11. Your dish is ready to be served.

2.5 Indian Spiced Omelet Recipe

Preparation Time: 10 minutes
Cooking Time: 30 minutes
Serving: 2

Ingredients:

- Eggs, four
- Onions, two
- Olive oil, two tablespoon
- Ginger, one teaspoon
- Tomatoes, two
- Garlic cloves, four
- Green chilies, three
- Salt, to taste
- Black pepper, to taste
- Coriander leaves, one teaspoon
- Garam Masala, half teaspoon
- Black mustard seeds, one teaspoon
- Chopped coriander, for garnishing
- Cumin seeds, one teaspoon

Instructions:
1. Take a large bowl.
2. Add all the ingredients into the bowl.

3. Mix the ingredients carefully.
4. Add the mixture in small quantities in a pan.
5. Let the omelet turn golden on both sides.
6. Add a little chopped coriander on top of the omelet.
7. Your dish is ready to be served.

2.6 Indian Poha Recipe

Preparation Time: 10 minutes
Cooking Time: 30 minutes
Serving: 4

Ingredients:

- Poha, one cup
- Oil, two tablespoon
- Potato, one
- Mustard seeds, one teaspoon
- Curry leaves, two
- Onions, one
- Turmeric powder, one teaspoon
- Salt, to taste
- Sugar, to taste
- Red peanuts, half cup
- Coriander leaves, two
- Lemon, one
- Green chilies, four to five

Instructions:
1. Heat the oil in a pan.
2. Add the potato and fry it.
3. Wash the poha and add it in the pan.
4. Cook the poha along with fried potato.

5. Add the onions, mustard seeds and curry leaves into cooking mixture.
6. Add the peanut, green chilies and coriander leaves in it.
7. Add the lemon as required.
8. Cook the mixture for ten minutes.
9. Add the salt and sugar to taste.
10. Your dish is ready to be served.

2.7 Indian Aloo Puri Recipe

Preparation Time: 15 minutes
Cooking Time: 15 minutes
Serving: 2

Ingredients:

- Oil, for frying
- Sooji, half cup
- Mashed potatoes, two cups
- Flour, two cups
- Cumin seeds, one teaspoon
- Chopped ginger, half tablespoon
- Salt, to taste
- Turmeric powder, one teaspoon
- Green chutney, half cup
- Onion, one

Instructions:
1. Take a large bowl and add the sooji and flour into it.
2. Add the mashed potatoes and cumin seeds into it.
3. Add the salt, pepper and chopped cilantro in it.
4. Add the chopped onions and turmeric powder.

5. Mix them well.
6. Add some oil to make dough of it.
7. Make round balls of the formed dough.
8. Dust the balls with wheat flour and roll them to make a round roti.
9. Cook the rolled puri on a hot pan full of oil.
10. Cook the puri well.
11. Your dish is ready to be served with green chutney.

2.8 Indian Scrambled Eggs Recipe

Preparation Time: 10 minutes
Cooking Time: 30 minutes
Serving: 2

Ingredients:

- Eggs, four
- Onions, two
- Olive oil, two tablespoon
- Water, two cups
- Ginger, one teaspoon
- Tomatoes, two
- Garlic cloves, four
- Green chilies, three
- Salt, to taste
- Black pepper, to taste
- Coriander leaves, one teaspoon
- Garam Masala, half teaspoon
- Black mustard seeds, one teaspoon
- Chopped coriander, for garnishing
- Cumin seeds, one teaspoon

Instructions:
1. Heat a pan.
2. Add the oil into the pan.
3. Add the garlic and onions.
4. Add in the tomato cook until delicate however to some degree crispy.
5. Turn down the warmth and pour the beaten eggs and leave to set for a couple of moments.
6. Scramble the egg mixture and add the rest of the ingredients.
7. Add some salt and pepper.
8. Garnish it with chopped coriander leaves.
9. Your dish is ready to be served.

2.9 Indian Oats Kheer Recipe

Preparation Time: 20 minutes
Cooking Time: 20 minutes
Serving: 4

Ingredients:

- Pure ghee, two tablespoon
- Condensed milk, two tablespoon
- Sugar, one cup
- Milk, one and half cup
- Oats, two cup
- Raisins, one cup
- Chopped cashew nuts, one cup
- Cardamom powder, one teaspoon

Instructions:
1. Take a large pan.
2. Add the pure ghee into it.

3. Add the oats into the ghee.
4. Fry the oats for about five minutes.
5. Add the sugar into the mixture and melt the sugar.
6. Add the milk and rest of the ingredients into the mixture.
7. Cook the kheer for about fifteen to twenty minutes.
8. The dish is ready to be served.

2.10 Indian Rava Idli Recipe

Preparation Time: 20 minutes
Cooking Time: 20 minutes
Serving: 4

Ingredients:

- Rava, one cup
- Chopped onion, one
- Green chili, two
- Ginger powder, one teaspoon
- Curry leaves, two
- Idli rice, one cup
- Urad dal, half teaspoon
- Oil, two tablespoon
- Salt, to taste
- Chopped coriander leaves, one tablespoon

Instructions:
1. Roast the rava and idli rice in a pan until it becomes light brown in color.
2. Heat the oil in another pan.

3. Add the mustard seeds, urad dal, and curry leaves in it.
4. Cook them well.
5. Add the onions, green chilies and ginger into it.
6. Cook it until the onions become golden brown in color.
7. Add water and cook the ingredients well.
8. Add the salt and pepper to taste.
9. Your dish is ready to be served.

Chapter 3: The World of Indian Lunch Recipes

Indian lunch recipes are full of flavors. There are many varieties of Indian dishes that can be eaten during the lunch time. Following are some easy to make recipes that you can cook today:

3.1 Indian Curry Oatmeal with Tandoori Masala Roasted Zucchini Recipe

Preparation Time: 10 minutes
Cooking Time: 30 minutes
Serving: 2

Ingredients:

- Oatmeal, one cup
- Onions, two
- Olive oil, two tablespoon
- Water, two cups
- Ginger, one teaspoon
- Tomatoes, two
- Garlic cloves, four
- Green chilies, three
- Salt, to taste
- Black pepper, to taste
- Zucchini pieces, two cups
- Coriander leaves, one teaspoon
- Garam Masala, half teaspoon
- Black mustard seeds, one teaspoon
- Cumin seeds, one teaspoon

Instructions:

1. Take a pan and add the oil in it.
2. Heat the oil and add onions in it.
3. Cook the onions until they become light brown in color.
4. Add the cumin seeds and mustard seeds in the pan.
5. Cook them well and add the salt and pepper and green chilies.
6. Add the turmeric, ginger and garlic cloves in it.
7. Mix them well and continue cooking.
8. Add some water if needed.
9. Add the oats into the cooking mixture.
10. Add the coriander leaves and garam masala as needed.
11. Mix all the ingredients and cook for few minutes.
12. Add the water according to the quantity of curry you want.
13. Roast the zucchini in the oven for ten minutes and add it into the curry.
14. Your dish is ready to be served.

3.2 Indian Chicken Biryani Recipes

Preparation Time: 10 minutes
Cooking Time: 30 minutes
Serving: 4

Ingredients:

- Rice, two cups
- Chicken pieces, one pound
- Olive oil, two tablespoon
- Water, two cups
- Ginger, one teaspoon
- Tomatoes, two
- Garlic cloves, four
- Green chilies, three
- Salt, to taste
- Black pepper, to taste
- Coriander leaves, one teaspoon
- Garam Masala, half teaspoon
- Black mustard seeds, one teaspoon
- Cumin seeds, one teaspoon
- Onions, two

Instructions:
1. Take a pan and add the oil in it.
2. Heat the oil and add onions in it.
3. Fry the onions until they become light brown in color.
4. Add the cumin seeds, peas and mustard seeds in the pan.
5. Fry them well and add the salt and pepper and green chilies.
6. Add the turmeric, ginger and garlic cloves in it.

7. Mix them well and continue cooking.
8. Add the chicken in the cooking mixture.
9. Cook all the ingredients until they become tender.
10. Add the coriander leaves and garam masala as needed.
11. Mix all the ingredients and cook for few minutes.
12. Boil the rice in water until they become eatable.
13. Pour the prepared masala over rice in layers.
14. Your dish is ready to be served.

3.3 Indian Naan Pizza with Roasted Chicken Recipe

Preparation Time: 20 minutes
Cooking Time: 10 minutes
Serving: 4

Ingredients:

- Oil, two tablespoon
- Cumin seeds, one teaspoon
- Chopped ginger, half tablespoon
- Roasted chicken, two cups
- Cheese, one cup
- Salt, to taste
- Chopped coriander leaves, two
- Naan, four
- Green chutney, half cup
- Tomato, one
- Capsicum rings, five
- Butter, two tablespoon

Instructions:
1. Take a pan and heat the oil in it.
2. Add the onions, tomatoes and fry them well.
3. Add the salt, pepper and chopped cilantro in it.
4. Add the chopped ginger, chicken and turmeric in it.
5. Mix them well.
6. Take the naan and spread the butter on it.
7. Spread the chicken mixture over it.
8. Top it with capsicum rings and sprinkle the cheese on top.
9. Bake your naan in the oven.
10. Your dish is ready to be served.

3.4 Indian Capsicum Rice Recipe

Preparation Time: 10 minutes
Cooking Time: 30 minutes
Serving: 4

Ingredients:

- Rice, two cups
- Capsicum, two cups
- Olive oil, two tablespoon
- Water, two cups
- Ginger, one teaspoon
- Tomatoes, two
- Garlic cloves, four
- Green chilies, three
- Salt, to taste
- Black pepper, to taste
- Coriander leaves, one teaspoon
- Garam Masala, half teaspoon

- Black mustard seeds, one teaspoon
- Cumin seeds, one teaspoon
- Onions, two

Instructions:
1. Take a pan and add the oil in it.
2. Heat the oil and add onions in it.
3. Fry the onions until they become light brown in color.
4. Add the cumin seeds, capsicum and mustard seeds in the pan.
5. Fry them well and add the salt and pepper and green chilies.
6. Add the turmeric, ginger and garlic cloves in it.
7. Mix them well and continue cooking.
8. Cook all the vegetables until they become tender.
9. Add the coriander leaves and garam masala as needed.
10. Mix all the ingredients and cook for few minutes.
11. Boil the rice in water until they become soft.
12. Pour the prepared masala over the rice.
13. Your dish is ready to be served.

3.5 Indian Aval Upma Recipe

Preparation Time: 10 minutes
Cooking Time: 20 minutes
Serving: 4

Ingredients:

- Chopped bread cubes, two cups
- Oil, two tablespoon
- Mustard seeds, one teaspoon
- Cumin seeds, one teaspoon
- Onions, one
- Tomatoes, two
- Green chili, Two
- Ginger powder, one tablespoon
- Turmeric powder, half teaspoon
- Red chili powder, half teaspoon
- Curry leaves, five
- Chopped coriander leaves, one tablespoon
- Salt, to taste
- Black pepper, to taste

Instructions:
1. Chop the bread well into slices.
2. Chop the onions, tomatoes, green chili and Ginger.
3. Add all the above ingredients into a large bowl.
4. Chop the curry leaves and coriander leaves.
5. Keep the leaves aside in a bowl.
6. Heat the oil in a pan and add the mustard seeds in it.

7. Add the cumin seeds and cook it until the color of the seeds change.
8. Add the onions into it.
9. Add the chopped tomatoes and green chili.
10. Add the ginger powder and mix the ingredients well.
11. Add the turmeric powder and red chili powder.
12. Mix very well and add salt.
13. Cook the ingredients well until no moisture is left.
14. In the end add the bread cubes and mix it with the cooked mixture.
15. Cook it for five minutes.
16. Add the coriander leaves and curry leaves into the bread mixture.
17. Your dish is ready to be served.

3.6 Indian Style Chicken and Onions Recipe

Preparation Time: 10 minutes
Cooking Time: 20 minutes
Serving: 2

Ingredients:

- Chicken pieces, one pound
- Cumin seeds, one tablespoon
- Onions, two
- Olive oil, two tablespoon
- Water, two cups
- Ginger, one teaspoon
- Tomatoes, two
- Garlic cloves, four

- Green chilies, three
- Salt, to taste
- Black pepper, to taste
- Coriander leaves, one teaspoon
- Garam Masala, half teaspoon
- Black mustard seeds, one teaspoon
- Indian black salt, one tablespoon

Instructions:
1. Take a pan and add the oil in it.
2. Heat the oil and add onions in it.
3. Fry the onions until they become light brown in color.
4. Add the cumin seeds and mustard seeds in the pan.
5. Fry them well and add the salt and pepper and green chilies.
6. Add the turmeric, ginger and garlic cloves in it.
7. Mix them well and continue cooking.
8. Add some water if needed.
9. Add the chicken into the cooking mixture.
10. Add the coriander leaves and garam masala as needed.
11. Mix all the ingredients and cook for few minutes.
12. Add the Indian black salt for taste.
13. Your dish is ready to be served.

3.7 Indian Tomato Rice Recipe

Preparation Time: 10 minutes
Cooking Time: 30 minutes
Serving: 4

Ingredients:

- Rice, two cups
- Tomato puree, two cups
- Olive oil, two tablespoon
- Water, two cups
- Ginger, one teaspoon
- Tomatoes, two
- Garlic cloves, four
- Green chilies, three
- Salt, to taste
- Black pepper, to taste
- Coriander leaves, one teaspoon
- Garam Masala, half teaspoon
- Black mustard seeds, one teaspoon
- Cumin seeds, one teaspoon
- Onions, two

Instructions:
1. Take a pan and add the oil in it.
2. Heat the oil and add onions in it.
3. Fry the onions until they become light brown in color.
4. Add the cumin seeds, tomatoes and mustard seeds in the pan.

5. Fry them well and add the salt and pepper and green chilies.
6. Add the turmeric, tomato puree, ginger and garlic cloves in it.
7. Mix them well and continue cooking.
8. Add the coriander leaves and garam masala as needed.
9. Mix all the ingredients and cook for few minutes.
10. Boil the rice in water until they become soft.
11. Pour the prepared masala over the rice.
12. Your dish is ready to be served.

3.8 Indian Chicken Curry Recipe

Preparation Time: 10 minutes
Cooking Time: 30 minutes
Serving: 2

Ingredients:

- Chicken pieces, half pound
- Onions, two
- Olive oil, two tablespoon
- Water, two cups
- Ginger, one teaspoon
- Tomatoes, two
- Garlic cloves, four
- Green chilies, three
- Salt, to taste
- Black pepper, to taste
- Coriander leaves, one teaspoon
- Garam Masala, half teaspoon
- Black mustard seeds, one teaspoon
- Cumin seeds, one teaspoon

Instructions:
1. Take a pan and add the oil in it.
2. Heat the oil and add onions in it.
3. Fry the onions until they become light brown in color.
4. Add the cumin seeds and mustard seeds in the pan.
5. Fry them well and add the salt and pepper and green chilies.
6. Add the turmeric, ginger and garlic cloves in it.
7. Mix them well and continue cooking.
8. Add some water if needed.
9. Add the chicken pieces into the cooking mixture.
10. Add the coriander leaves and garam masala as needed.
11. Mix all the ingredients and cook for few minutes.
12. Add the water according to the quantity of curry you want.
13. Cook it until the chicken becomes soft.
14. Your dish is ready to be served.

3.9 Indian Butter Chicken Recipe

Preparation Time: 10 minutes
Cooking Time: 30 minutes
Serving: 2

Ingredients:

- Chicken pieces, half pound
- Onions, two
- Unsalted butter, half cup
- Ginger, one teaspoon
- Tomatoes, two
- Garlic cloves, four
- Green chilies, three
- Salt, to taste
- Black pepper, to taste
- Cream, half cup
- Coriander leaves, one teaspoon
- Garam Masala, half teaspoon
- Black mustard seeds, one teaspoon
- Cumin seeds, one teaspoon

Instructions:
1. Take a pan and add the butter in it.
2. Heat the oil and add onions in it.
3. Fry the onions until they become light brown in color.
4. Add the cumin seeds and mustard seeds in the pan.
5. Fry them well and add the salt and pepper and green chilies.
6. Add the turmeric, ginger and garlic cloves in it.
7. Mix them well and continue cooking.

8. Add the chicken pieces and cream into the cooking mixture.
9. Add the coriander leaves and garam masala as needed.
10. Mix all the ingredients and cook for few minutes.
11. Cook it until the chicken becomes soft.
12. Your dish is ready to be served.

3.10 Indian Chili Chicken Recipe

Preparation Time: 20 minutes
Cooking Time: 20 minutes
Serving: 4

Ingredients:

- Garam masala, two tablespoon
- Chopped red chilies, two tablespoon
- Chicken pieces, one pound
- Tomatoes, two
- Red chili powder, one tablespoon
- Oil, three tablespoon
- Garlic cloves, three
- Ginger, two tablespoon
- Chopped coriander leaves, one teaspoon
- Sea salt, two teaspoon
- Chopped cilantro, one cup
- Chopped onions, two tablespoon

Instructions:
1. Take a skillet and add the oil in it.
2. Heat the oil and add onions in it.

3. Fry the onions until they become light brown in color.
4. Add the red chilies in the skillet.
5. Fry them well and add the salt and pepper and green chilies.
6. Add the turmeric, ginger and garlic cloves in it.
7. Mix them well and continue cooking.
8. Add some water if needed.
9. Add the coriander leaves and chopped tomatoes as needed.
10. Mix all the ingredients and cook for few minutes.
11. Add chicken once the mixture is cooked.
12. Add chopped cilantro and cayenne powder to taste.
13. Cook it until the chicken becomes soft.
14. Your dish is ready to be served.

3.11 Indian Cashew Chicken Recipe

Preparation Time: 10 minutes
Cooking Time: 30 minutes
Serving: 2

Ingredients:

- Chicken pieces, half pound
- Onions, two
- Unsalted butter, half cup
- Ginger, one teaspoon
- Tomatoes, two
- Garlic cloves, four
- Green chilies, three
- Salt, to taste

- Black pepper, to taste
- Cashew nuts, one cup
- Garam Masala, half teaspoon
- Black mustard seeds, one teaspoon
- Cumin seeds, one teaspoon

Instructions:
1. Take a pan and add oil in it.
2. Heat the oil and add onions in it.
3. Fry the onions until they become light brown in color.
4. Add the cumin seeds and mustard seeds in the pan.
5. Fry them well and add the salt and pepper and green chilies.
6. Add the turmeric, ginger and garlic cloves in it.
7. Mix them well and continue cooking.
8. Add the chicken pieces into the cooking mixture.
9. Add the cashew nuts and garam masala as needed.
10. Mix all the ingredients and cook for few minutes.
11. Cook them until the chicken becomes soft.
12. Your dish is ready to be served.

3.12 Indian Paneer Burji Recipe

Preparation Time: 30 minutes
Cooking Time: 10 minutes
Serving: 4

Ingredients:

- Garam masala, two tablespoon
- Paneer, two cups
- Tomatoes, two
- Red chili powder, one tablespoon
- Oil, three tablespoon
- Garlic cloves, three
- Ginger, two tablespoon
- Cumin seeds, one teaspoon
- Chopped coriander leaves, one teaspoon
- Sea salt, two teaspoon
- Chopped cilantro, one cup
- Chopped onions, two tablespoon
- Indian black salt, to taste

Instructions:
1. Take a skillet and add oil in it.
2. Heat the oil and add onions in it.
3. Fry the onions until they become light brown in color.
4. Add the cumin seeds in the skillet.
5. Add the tomatoes and paneer into the mixture.
6. Fry them well and add the salt and pepper and green chilies.
7. Add the turmeric, ginger and garlic cloves in it.

8. Mix them well and continue cooking.
9. Add the chopped tomatoes and Indian black salt in the mixture.
10. Add the coriander leaves and garam masala as needed.
11. Mix all the ingredients and cook for few minutes.
12. Your dish is ready to be served.

3.13 Indian Chicken Tikka Masala Recipe

Preparation Time: 20 minutes
Cooking Time: 20 minutes
Serving: 4

Ingredients:

- Tikka masala, two tablespoon
- Chicken pieces, one pound
- Tomatoes, two
- Red chili powder, one tablespoon
- Oil, three tablespoon
- Garlic cloves, three
- Ginger, two tablespoon
- Chopped coriander leaves, one teaspoon
- Sea salt, two teaspoon
- Chopped cilantro, one cup
- Chopped onions, two tablespoon

Instructions:
1. Take a skillet and add oil in it.
2. Heat the oil and add onions in it.
3. Fry the onions until they become light brown in color.

4. Add the red chilies in the skillet.
5. Fry them well and add the salt and pepper and green chilies.
6. Add the turmeric, ginger and garlic cloves in it.
7. Mix them well and continue cooking.
8. Add the tikka masala and chopped tomatoes as needed.
9. Mix all the ingredients and cook for few minutes.
10. Add chicken once the mixture is cooked.
11. Cook them until the chicken becomes soft.
12. Your dish is ready to be served.

3.14 Indian Cauliflower Tikka Masala Curry Recipe

Preparation Time: 20 minutes
Cooking Time: 20 minutes
Serving: 4

Ingredients:

- Tikka masala, two tablespoon
- Cauliflower florets, one pound
- Tomatoes, two
- Red chili powder, one tablespoon
- Oil, three tablespoon
- Garlic cloves, three
- Ginger, two tablespoon
- Chopped coriander leaves, one teaspoon
- Sea salt, two teaspoon
- Chopped cilantro, one cup
- Chopped onions, two tablespoon

Instructions:

1. Take a skillet and add oil in it.
2. Heat the oil and add onions in it.
3. Fry the onions until they become light brown in color.
4. Add the red chilies in the skillet.
5. Fry them well and add the salt, pepper and green chilies.
6. Add the turmeric, ginger and garlic cloves in it.
7. Mix them well and continue cooking.
8. Add the tikka masala and chopped tomatoes as needed.
9. Mix all the ingredients and cook for few minutes.
10. Add cauliflower once the mixture is cooked.
11. Your dish is ready to be served.

3.15 Indian Roasted Vegetables Recipe

Preparation Time: 10 minutes
Cooking Time: 25 minutes
Serving: 2

Ingredients:

- Potatoes, half cup
- Oil, two tablespoon
- Dhal, one cup
- Onion, one cup
- Cauliflower, one cup

- Water, one cup
- Minced garlic, two tablespoon
- Minced ginger, two tablespoon
- Tomato, two
- Cumin seeds, one teaspoon
- Coriander leaves, one
- Indian black salt, to taste
- Green chilies, two
- Garam masala, one tablespoon

Instructions:
1. Take a skillet and add oil in it.
2. Heat the oil and add onions in it.
3. Fry the onions until they become light brown in color.
4. Add the cumin seeds in the skillet.
5. Fry them well and add the salt, pepper and green chilies.
6. Add the turmeric, ginger and garlic cloves in it.
7. Mix them well and continue cooking.
8. Add the coriander leaves and chopped tomatoes as needed.
9. Mix all the ingredients and cook for few minutes.
10. Add the cauliflower once the mixture is cooked.

11. Bake the cauliflower mixture for about ten minutes.
12. Your dish is ready to be served.

3.16 Indian Moong Daal Kichri Recipe

Preparation Time: 10 minutes
Cooking Time: 20 minutes
Serving: 4

Ingredients:

- Daal, one cup
- Rice, one cup
- Lemon, four to five
- Cumin seeds, one tablespoon
- Onions, two
- Olive oil, two tablespoon
- Water, two cups
- Ginger, one teaspoon
- Tomatoes, two
- Garlic cloves, four
- Green chilies, three
- Salt, to taste
- Black pepper, to taste
- Coriander leaves, one teaspoon
- Garam Masala, half teaspoon
- Black mustard seeds, one teaspoon

Instructions:
1. Take a pan and add the oil in it.
2. Heat the oil and add onions in it.

3. Fry the onions until they become light brown in color.
4. Add the cumin seeds and mustard seeds in the pan.
5. Fry them well and add the salt and pepper and green chilies.
6. Add the turmeric, daal, ginger and garlic cloves in it.
7. Mix them well and continue cooking.
8. Add some water if needed.
9. Add the lemon pieces into the cooking mixture.
10. Add the coriander leaves and garam masala as needed.
11. Mix all the ingredients and cook for few minutes.
12. When the masala is prepared, add the water triple of rice quantity.
13. Add the rice in boiling water with all ingredients.
14. Cook them until no water is left.
15. Cover the pan with lid and leave it for ten minutes on low heat.
16. Your dish is ready to be served.

3.17 Indian Rajma Chawal Recipe

Preparation Time: 10 minutes
Cooking Time: 30 minutes
Serving: 4

Ingredients:

- Rice, two cups
- Red beans, two cups
- Olive oil, two tablespoon
- Water, two cups
- Ginger, one teaspoon
- Tomatoes, two
- Garlic cloves, four
- Green chilies, three
- Salt, to taste
- Black pepper, to taste
- Coriander leaves, one teaspoon
- Garam Masala, half teaspoon
- Black mustard seeds, one teaspoon
- Cumin seeds, one teaspoon
- Onions, two

Instructions:
1. Take a pan and add the oil in it.
2. Heat the oil and add onions in it.
3. Fry the onions until they become light brown in color.
4. Add the cumin seeds, tomatoes and mustard seeds in the pan.
5. Fry them well and add the salt and pepper and green chilies.

6. Add the turmeric, red beans, ginger and garlic cloves in it.
7. Mix them well and continue cooking.
8. Add the coriander leaves and garam masala as needed.
9. Mix all the ingredients and cook for few minutes.
10. Boil the rice in water until they become soft.
11. Pour the prepared masala over the rice.
12. Your dish is ready to be served.

3.18 Indian Mattar Paneer Recipe

Preparation Time: 30 minutes
Cooking Time: 10 minutes
Serving: 4

Ingredients:

- Garam masala, two tablespoon
- Paneer, two cups
- Tomatoes, two
- Red chili powder, one tablespoon
- Oil, three tablespoon
- Garlic cloves, three
- Peas, one cup
- Ginger, two tablespoon
- Cumin seeds, one teaspoon
- Chopped coriander leaves, one teaspoon
- Sea salt, two teaspoon
- Chopped cilantro, one cup
- Chopped onions, two tablespoon
- Indian black salt, to taste

Instructions:
1. Take a skillet and add the oil in it.
2. Heat the oil and add onions in it.
3. Fry the onions until they become light brown in color.
4. Add the cumin seeds in the skillet.
5. Add the tomatoes, peas and paneer into the mixture.
6. Fry them well and add the salt and pepper and green chilies.
7. Add the turmeric, ginger and garlic cloves in it.
8. Mix them well and continue cooking.
9. Add the chopped tomatoes and Indian black salt in the mixture.
10. Add the coriander leaves and garam masala as needed.
11. Mix all the ingredients and cook for few minutes.
12. Your dish is ready to be served.

3.19 Indian Paneer Tikka Masala Recipe

Preparation Time: 20 minutes
Cooking Time: 20 minutes
Serving: 4

Ingredients:

- Tikka masala, two tablespoon
- Paneer pieces, one pound
- Tomatoes, two
- Red chili powder, one tablespoon
- Oil, three tablespoon
- Garlic cloves, three
- Ginger, two tablespoon
- Chopped coriander leaves, one teaspoon
- Sea salt, two teaspoon
- Chopped cilantro, one cup
- Chopped onions, two tablespoon

Instructions:
1. Take a skillet and add the oil in it.
2. Heat the oil and add onions in it.
3. Fry the onions until they become light brown in color.
4. Add the red chilies in the skillet.
5. Fry them well and add the salt and pepper and green chilies.
6. Add the turmeric, ginger and garlic cloves in it.
7. Mix them well and continue cooking.
8. Add the tikka masala and chopped tomatoes as needed.
9. Mix all the ingredients and cook for few minutes.

10. Add the paneer cubes once the mixture is cooked.
11. Cook it until paneer become soft.
12. Your dish is ready to be served.

3.20 Indian Spiced Vegetable Burger Recipe

Preparation Time: 15 minutes
Cooking Time: 20 minutes
Serving: 4

Ingredients:

- Minced mixed vegetables, one cup
- Egg, one
- Bread crumbs, one cup
- Mix Indian spices, one teaspoon
- Chopped onion, half cup
- Chopped tomatoes, half cup
- Chopped coriander, a quarter cup
- Burger buns, four
- Cooking oil, for frying
- Ketchup, as required

Instructions:
1. Take a large bowl.
2. Add all the filling ingredients into a bowl.
3. Mix all the ingredients well and form patties.
4. Fry the patties in a large pan.
5. Toast the buns and add the patty and ketchup on top of the buns.
6. The dish is ready to be served.

Chapter 4: The World of Indian Dinner Recipes

Indian dinner recipes are well- known all over the world for its mesmerizing flavors and varieties. Following are some amazing and healthy Indian dinner recipes that you would love to make at home:

4.1 Indian Chicken Qorma Recipe

Preparation Time: 10 minutes
Cooking Time: 20 minutes
Serving: 2

Ingredients:

- Chicken pieces, one pound
- Cumin seeds, one tablespoon
- Onions, two
- Yoghurt, half cup
- Cardamom, four
- Olive oil, two tablespoon
- Ginger, one teaspoon
- Tomatoes, two
- Garlic cloves, four
- Green chilies, three
- Salt, to taste
- Black pepper, to taste
- Coriander leaves, one teaspoon
- Garam Masala, half teaspoon
- Black mustard seeds, one teaspoon
- Indian black salt, one tablespoon

Instructions:
1. Take a large bowl.
2. Add the chicken, yoghurt and spices into it.
3. Mix everything together and keep it aside.
4. Add the oil and cardamom into a large pan.
5. Cook the onions and then add the ginger and garlic.
6. Cook the ingredients for a few minutes and then add the tomatoes.
7. Cook the tomatoes until they melt away.
8. Add the chicken and mix.
9. Cook the dish on high heat and then reduce the flame to low.
10. Cover the pan with a lid.
11. Cook for ten to fifteen minutes.
12. Your dish is ready to be served.

4.2 Indian Dum Aloo Recipe

Preparation Time: 10 minutes
Cooking Time: 20 minutes
Serving: 2

Ingredients:

- Potato pieces, one pound
- Cumin seeds, one tablespoon
- Onions, two
- Cream, half cup
- Cardamom, four
- Olive oil, two tablespoon
- Water, two cups
- Ginger, one teaspoon
- Tomatoes, two

- Garlic cloves, four
- Green chilies, three
- Salt, to taste
- Black pepper, to taste
- Coriander leaves, one teaspoon
- Garam Masala, half teaspoon
- Black mustard seeds, one teaspoon
- Indian black salt, one tablespoon

Instructions:
1. Add the oil and cardamom into a large pan.
2. Cook the onions and then add the ginger and garlic.
3. Cook the ingredients for a few minutes and then add the tomatoes.
4. Cook the tomatoes until they are soft.
5. Add the potatoes and mix.
6. Add the cream after a while.
7. Cook the dish on high heat and then reduce the flame to low.
8. Cover the pan with a lid.
9. Cook for ten to fifteen minutes.
10. Your dish is ready to be served.

4.3 Indian Palak Paneer Recipe

Preparation Time: 30 minutes
Cooking Time: 10 minutes
Serving: 4

Ingredients:

- Garam masala, two tablespoon
- Paneer, two cups
- Tomatoes, two
- Red chili powder, one tablespoon
- Oil, three tablespoon
- Garlic cloves, three
- Spinach leaves (palak), one cup
- Ginger, two tablespoon
- Cumin seeds, one teaspoon
- Chopped coriander leaves, one teaspoon
- Sea salt, two teaspoon
- Chopped cilantro, one cup
- Chopped onions, two tablespoon
- Indian black salt, to taste

Instructions:
1. Take a skillet and add the oil in it.
2. Heat the oil and add onions in it.
3. Fry the onions until they become light brown in color.
4. Add the cumin seeds in the skillet.
5. Add the tomatoes, palak and paneer into the mixture.
6. Fry them well and add the salt and pepper and green chilies.

7. Add the turmeric, ginger and garlic cloves in it.
8. Mix them well and continue cooking.
9. Add the chopped tomatoes and Indian black salt in the mixture.
10. Add the coriander leaves and garam masala as needed.
11. Mix all the ingredients and cook for few minutes.
12. Your dish is ready to be served.

4.4 Indian Tamarind Rice Recipe

Preparation Time: 10 minutes
Cooking Time: 30 minutes
Serving: 4

Ingredients:

- Rice, two cups
- Tamarind paste, two cups
- Olive oil, two tablespoon
- Water, two cups
- Ginger, one teaspoon
- Tomatoes, two
- Garlic cloves, four
- Green chilies, three
- Salt, to taste
- Black pepper, to taste
- Coriander leaves, one teaspoon
- Garam Masala, half teaspoon
- Black mustard seeds, one teaspoon
- Cumin seeds, one teaspoon
- Onions, two

Instructions:
1. Take a pan and add the oil in it.
2. Heat the oil and add onions in it.
3. Fry the onions until they become light brown in color.
4. Add the cumin seeds, tomatoes and mustard seeds in the pan.
5. Fry them well and add the salt and pepper and green chilies.
6. Add the turmeric, tamarind paste, ginger and garlic cloves in it.
7. Mix them well and continue cooking.
8. Add the coriander leaves and garam masala as needed.
9. Mix all the ingredients and cook for few minutes.
10. Boil the rice in water until they become soft.
11. Pour the prepared masala over the rice.
12. Your dish is ready to be served.

4.5 Indian Samber Recipe

Preparation Time: 15 minutes
Cooking Time: 20 minutes
Serving: 4

Ingredients:

- Lentil, half pound
- Samber powder, three teaspoon
- Oil, three tablespoon
- Garlic cloves, three
- Ginger, two tablespoon
- Cumin seeds, one teaspoon

- Chopped coriander leaves, one teaspoon
- Cayenne powder, one teaspoon
- Jaggery, one tablespoon
- Okra, one cup
- Tamarind paste, two tablespoon
- Sea salt, two teaspoon
- Chopped cilantro, one cup
- Garam masala, two tablespoon
- Chopped tomatoes, one cup

Instructions:
1. Take a pan.
2. Add in the oil and onions.
3. Cook the onions until they become soft and fragrant.
4. Add in the chopped garlic and ginger.
5. Cook the mixture and add the tomatoes into it.
6. Add the spices and salt.
7. Add the coriander leaves and garam masala.
8. Add the rest of the ingredients and cook for ten to fifteen minutes.
9. The dish is ready to be served.

4.6 Indian Daal Fry Recipe

Preparation Time: 10 minutes
Cooking Time: 25 minutes
Serving: 2

Ingredients:

- Coconut oil, two tablespoon

- Lentil, one cup
- Onions, one
- Garlic cloves, three
- Ginger, two tablespoon
- Cumin seeds, one teaspoon
- Chopped coriander leaves, one teaspoon
- Cayenne powder, one teaspoon
- Sea salt, two teaspoon
- Chopped cilantro, one cup
- Coconut milk, half cup
- Tomatoes, one
- Brown sugar, two tablespoon

Instructions:
1. Take a skillet and add the coconut oil in it.
2. Heat the oil and add onions in it.
3. Fry the onions until they become light brown in color.
4. Add the cumin seeds in the skillet.
5. Fry them well and add the salt and pepper and green chilies.
6. Add the turmeric, ginger and garlic cloves in it.
7. Mix them well and continue cooking.
8. Add some water if needed.
9. Add the coriander leaves and chopped tomatoes as needed.
10. Mix all the ingredients and cook for few minutes.
11. Add the coconut milk once the mixture is cooked.
12. Add chopped cilantro and cayenne powder to taste.
13. Add the roasted lentils in the end.
14. Add the brown sugar as needed.

15. Your dish is ready to be served.

4.7 Indian Parippu Curry Recipe

Preparation Time: 10 minutes
Cooking Time: 30 minutes
Serving: 2

Ingredients:

- Kerela pieces, half pound
- Onions, two
- Olive oil, two tablespoon
- Water, two cups
- Ginger, one teaspoon
- Tomatoes, two
- Garlic cloves, four
- Green chilies, three
- Salt, to taste
- Black pepper, to taste
- Coriander leaves, one teaspoon
- Cream, one cup
- Garam Masala, half teaspoon
- Black mustard seeds, one teaspoon
- Cumin seeds, one teaspoon

Instructions:
1. Take a pan and add the oil in it.
2. Heat the oil and add onions in it.
3. Fry the onions until they become light brown in color.
4. Add the cumin seeds and mustard seeds in the pan.

5. Fry them well and add the salt and pepper and green chilies.
6. Add the turmeric, ginger and garlic cloves in it.
7. Mix them well and continue cooking.
8. Add the kerela pieces and cream into the cooking mixture.
9. Add the coriander leaves and garam masala as needed.
10. Mix all the ingredients and cook for few minutes.
11. Add the water according to the quantity of curry you want.
12. Your dish is ready to be served.

4.8 Indian Style Fried Fish Recipe

Preparation Time: 10 minutes
Cooking Time: 30 minutes
Serving: 2

Ingredients:

- Fish pieces, half pound
- Onion powder, two teaspoon
- Cooking oil, for frying
- Ginger powder, one teaspoon
- Chili powder, two teaspoon
- Garlic powder, one teaspoon
- Salt, to taste
- Black pepper, to taste
- Gram flour, one cup
- Garam Masala, half teaspoon
- Cumin powder, one teaspoon

Instructions:

1. Take a large bowl.
2. Add all the ingredients into the bowl.
3. Mix all the ingredients well.
4. Add the cooking oil into a large frying pan.
5. Add the fish pieces into the pan.
6. Cook the fish pieces until they turn golden brown.
7. Your dish is ready to be served.

4.9 Indian Kerela Barta Recipe

Preparation Time: 20 minutes
Cooking Time: 20 minutes
Serving: 4

Ingredients:

- Kerela, one cup
- Onions, one
- Garlic cloves, three
- Ginger, two tablespoon
- Cumin seeds, one teaspoon
- Chopped coriander leaves, one teaspoon
- Cayenne powder, one teaspoon
- Sea salt, two teaspoon
- Chopped cilantro, one cup
- Tomatoes, one
- Ground peanuts, half cup

Instructions:
1. Take a bowl and add the chopped onions in it.
2. Add the garlic, ginger and cumin seeds in it.
3. Add the cayenne powder, ground peanuts and tomatoes in it.

4. Add the chopped coriander leaves and salt as needed.
5. Mix all the ingredients to make a filling material.
6. Take the kerela and wash them properly.
7. Cut the kerela in longitudinal direction for filling.
8. Fill them with the prepared filling material.
9. Heat the oil in a pan.
10. Add the filled kerela into it.
11. Cook it for ten minutes.
12. The dish is ready to be served.

4.10 Indian Kofta Recipe

Preparation Time: 10 minutes
Cooking Time: 20 minutes
Serving: 2

Ingredients:

- Frozen chicken koftas (meat balls), one pound
- Cumin seeds, one tablespoon
- Onions, two
- Yoghurt, half cup
- Cardamom, four
- Olive oil, two tablespoon
- Ginger, one teaspoon
- Tomatoes, two
- Garlic cloves, four
- Green chilies, three
- Salt, to taste
- Black pepper, to taste
- Coriander leaves, one teaspoon
- Garam Masala, half teaspoon
- Black mustard seeds, one teaspoon

- Indian black salt, one tablespoon

Instructions:
1. Take a large bowl.
2. Add the chicken kofta, yoghurt and spices into it.
3. Mix everything together and keep it aside.
4. Add the oil and cardamom into a large pan.
5. Cook the onions and then add the ginger and garlic.
6. Cook the ingredients for a few minutes and then add the tomatoes.
7. Cook the tomatoes until they become soft.
8. Add the kofta and mix.
9. Cook the dish on high heat and then reduce the flame to low.
10. Cover the pan with a lid.
11. Cook for ten to fifteen minutes.
12. Your dish is ready to be served.

4.11 Indian Missi Roti Recipe

Preparation Time: 15 minutes
Cooking Time: 15 minutes
Serving: 2

Ingredients:

- Oil, five tablespoon
- Kasuri Methi, two teaspoon
- Corn flour, a quarter cup
- Whole flour, one cup
- Chickpea flour, one cup
- All-purpose flour, one cup

- Cumin seeds, one teaspoon
- Chopped ginger, half tablespoon
- Salt, to taste
- Turmeric powder, one teaspoon
- Green chutney, half cup
- Tomato, one

Instructions:
1. Take a large bowl and add all types of flour mentioned above into it.
2. Add the kasuri methi and cumin seeds into it.
3. Add the salt, pepper and chopped cilantro in it.
4. Add the rest of the ingredients.
5. Mix them well.
6. Add some oil to make dough of it.
7. Make round balls of the formed dough.
8. Dust the balls with wheat flour and roll them to make a round roti.
9. Cook the rolled paratha on the hot pan.
10. Drizzle the oil on top.
11. Cook the roti well.
12. Your dish is ready to be served with green chutney.

4.12 Indian Murgh Mussalam Recipe

Preparation Time: 20 minutes
Cooking Time: 20 minutes
Serving: 4

Ingredients:

- Nutmeg powder, one teaspoon
- Ginger paste, half tablespoon
- Mustard oil, five tablespoon
- Chicken pieces, one pound
- Onion paste, one tablespoon
- Garlic paste, half tablespoon
- Cumin powder, half teaspoon
- Garam masala, one tablespoon
- Green chilies, two tablespoon
- Turmeric powder, half teaspoon
- Red chili powder, two tablespoon
- Yoghurt, half cup
- Green cardamom, two

Instructions:
1. Take a pan.
2. Add in the oil and onions.
3. Cook the onions until they become soft and fragrant.
4. Add in the chopped garlic and ginger.
5. Add the turmeric powder, green cardamom, red chili powder, cumin powder and nutmeg powder.
6. Add the chicken pieces and rest of the ingredients.
7. Cook all the ingredients for about twenty minutes.
8. Your dish is ready to be served.

4.13 Indian Rongi Recipe

Preparation Time: 10 minutes
Cooking Time: 20 minutes
Serving: 2

Ingredients:

- White beans, one pound
- Cumin seeds, one tablespoon
- Onions, two
- Olive oil, two tablespoon
- Water, two cups
- Ginger, one teaspoon
- Tomatoes, two
- Garlic cloves, four
- Green chilies, three
- Salt, to taste
- Black pepper, to taste
- Coriander leaves, one teaspoon
- Garam Masala, half teaspoon
- Black mustard seeds, one teaspoon

- Indian black salt, one tablespoon

Instructions:
1. Take a pan and add the oil in it.
2. Heat the oil and add onions in it.
3. Fry the onions until they become light brown in color.
4. Add the cumin seeds and mustard seeds in the pan.
5. Fry them well and add the salt and pepper and green chilies.
6. Add the turmeric, ginger and garlic cloves in it.
7. Mix them well and continue cooking.
8. Add some water if needed.
9. Add the white beans and tomatoes into the cooking mixture.
10. Add the coriander leaves and garam masala as needed.
11. Mix all the ingredients and cook for few minutes.
12. Add the Indian black salt for taste.
13. Your dish is ready to be served.

4.14 Indian Shahi Paneer Recipe

Preparation Time: 10 minutes
Cooking Time: 30 minutes
Serving: 2

Ingredients:

- Paneer pieces, half pound
- Badaam pieces, one cup
- Cashew nuts (kaaju), one cup
- Onions, two
- Olive oil, two tablespoon
- Water, two cups
- Ginger, one teaspoon
- Tomatoes, two
- Garlic cloves, four
- Green chilies, three
- Salt, to taste
- Black pepper, to taste
- Heavy cream, one cup
- Garam Masala, half teaspoon
- Black mustard seeds, one teaspoon
- Cumin seeds, one teaspoon

Instructions:
1. Take a pan and add the oil in it.
2. Heat the oil and add onions in it.
3. Fry the onions until they become light brown in color.
4. Add the cumin seeds and mustard seeds in the pan.
5. Fry them well and add the salt and pepper and green chilies.

6. Add the turmeric, ginger and garlic cloves in it.
7. Mix them well and continue cooking.
8. Add some water if needed.
9. Add the paneer pieces into the cooking mixture.
10. Add the heavy cream and garam masala as needed.
11. Mix all the ingredients and cook for few minutes.
12. Add the badaam and kaaju.
13. Your dish is ready to be served.

4.15 Indian Chetinadu Chicken Recipe

Preparation Time: 10 minutes
Cooking Time: 20 minutes
Serving: 2

Ingredients:

- Chicken pieces, one pound
- Cumin seeds, one tablespoon
- Onions, two
- Lemon juice, half cup
- Cardamom, four
- Olive oil, two tablespoon
- Water, two cups
- Ginger, one teaspoon
- Tomatoes, two
- Fresh desiccated coconut, half cup
- Garlic cloves, four
- Kashmiri red chili, two teaspoon
- Green chilies, three
- Salt, to taste
- Black pepper, to taste
- Coriander leaves, one teaspoon

- Garam Masala, half teaspoon
- Black mustard seeds, one teaspoon
- Indian black salt, one tablespoon

Instructions:
1. Take a large bowl.
2. Add the chicken and the spices into it.
3. Mix everything together and keep it aside.
4. Add the oil and cardamom into a large pan.
5. Cook the onions and then add the ginger and garlic.
6. Cook the ingredients for a few minutes.
7. Add the chicken and desiccated coconut into the pan.
8. Cook the dish on high heat and then reduce the flame to low.
9. Cover the pan with a lid.
10. Cook for ten to fifteen minutes.
11. Your dish is ready to be served.

4.16 Indian Fried Kerala and Beef Recipe

Preparation Time: 30 minutes
Cooking Time: 10 minutes
Serving: 4

Ingredients:

- Garam masala, two tablespoon
- Kerela, half pound
- Tomatoes, two
- Red chili powder, one tablespoon
- Oil, three tablespoon

- Beef chunks, half pound
- Garlic cloves, three
- Ginger, two tablespoon
- Cumin seeds, one teaspoon
- Chopped coriander leaves, one teaspoon
- Sea salt, two teaspoon
- Chopped cilantro, one cup
- Chopped onions, two tablespoon
- Indian black salt, to taste

Instructions:
1. Take a skillet and add the oil in it.
2. Heat the oil and add onions in it.
3. Fry the onions until they become light brown in color.
4. Add the cumin seeds in the skillet.
5. Add the beef and kerelas.
6. Fry them well and add the salt and pepper and green chilies.
7. Add the turmeric, ginger and garlic cloves in it.
8. Mix them well and continue cooking.
9. Add the chopped tomatoes and Indian black salt in the mixture.
10. Add the coriander leaves and garam masala as needed.
11. Mix all the ingredients and cook for few minutes.
12. Add chopped cilantro when tomatoes become soft.
13. Your dish is ready to be served.

4.17 Indian Sevai Recipe

Preparation Time: 30 minutes
Cooking Time: 10 minutes
Serving: 4

Ingredients:

- Rice sevai, two cups
- Oil, two tablespoon
- Mustard seeds, one teaspoon
- Cumin seeds, one teaspoon
- Green chilies, two
- Curry leaves, five
- Onion, one
- Beans, half cup
- Carrots chopped, half cup
- Chopped beans, half cup
- Fresh peas, half cup
- Tomato puree, half cup
- Turmeric powder, half teaspoon
- Roasted peanuts, two tablespoon
- Salt, to taste
- Black pepper, to taste
- Chopped garlic, half cup

Instructions:
1. Heat a pan and add the rice sevai in it.
2. Roast it for three to four minutes.
3. Heat the oil in another pan.
4. Add the mustard and cumin seeds.
5. Add the chilies and curry leaves, beans, carrots and peanuts in it.
6. Add the salt and black pepper as required.

7. Add the turmeric powder and onions in it.
8. Add the tomatoes and water in a pan.
9. Add the rice sevai and cook for five minutes.
10. Your dish is ready to be served.

4.18 Indian Stuffed Mushroom Recipe

Preparation Time: 20 minutes
Cooking Time: 20 minutes
Serving: 4

Ingredients:

- Mushrooms, one cup
- Onions, one
- Garlic cloves, three
- Ginger, two tablespoon
- Cumin seeds, one teaspoon
- Chopped coriander leaves, one teaspoon
- Cayenne powder, one teaspoon
- Sea salt, two teaspoon
- Chopped cilantro, one cup
- Tomatoes, one
- Ground peanuts, half cup

Instructions:
1. Take a bowl and add the chopped onions in it.
2. Add the garlic, ginger and cumin seeds in it.
3. Add the cayenne powder, ground peanuts and tomatoes in it.
4. Add the chopped coriander leaves and salt as needed.
5. Mix all the ingredients to make a filling material.
6. Take the mushroom and wash them properly.

7. Fill them with the prepared filling material.
8. Heat the oil in a pan.
9. Add the filled mushrooms into it.
10. Cook it for ten minutes.
11. The dish is ready to be served.

4.19 Indian Grilled Fish Recipe

Preparation Time: 10 minutes
Cooking Time: 30 minutes
Serving: 2

Ingredients:

- Fish pieces, half pound
- Onion powder, two teaspoon
- Cooking oil, for frying
- Ginger powder, one teaspoon
- Chili powder, two teaspoon
- Garlic powder, one teaspoon
- Salt, to taste
- Black pepper, to taste
- Garam Masala, half teaspoon
- Cumin powder, one teaspoon

Instructions:
1. Take a large bowl.
2. Add all the ingredients into the bowl.
3. Mix all the ingredients well.
4. Add the cooking oil into a large frying pan.
5. Add the fish pieces into the pan.
6. Grill the fish pieces until they turn golden brown.
7. Your dish is ready to be served.

4.20 Indian Mixed Vegetables Recipe

Preparation Time: 10 minutes
Cooking Time: 20 minutes
Serving: 2

Ingredients:

- Mixed vegetables, one pound
- Cumin seeds, one tablespoon
- Onions, two
- Yoghurt, half cup
- Cardamom, four
- Olive oil, two tablespoon
- Ginger, one teaspoon
- Tomatoes, two
- Garlic cloves, four
- Green chilies, three
- Salt, to taste
- Black pepper, to taste
- Coriander leaves, one teaspoon
- Garam Masala, half teaspoon
- Black mustard seeds, one teaspoon
- Indian black salt, one tablespoon

Instructions:
1. Take a large bowl.
2. Add the vegetables, yoghurt and spices into it.
3. Mix everything together and keep it aside.
4. Add the oil and cardamom into a large pan.
5. Cook the onions and then add the ginger and garlic.
6. Cook the ingredients for a few minutes and then add the tomatoes.

7. Cook the tomatoes until they become soft.
8. Add the vegetables and mix.
9. Cook the dish on high heat and then reduce the flame to low.
10. Cover the pan with a lid.
11. Cook for ten to fifteen minutes.
12. Your dish is ready to be served.

Chapter 5: The World of Indian Dessert Recipes

Indian desserts are well known throughout the world for their unique flavors. You should try all of these ten yummy dessert recipes at home as they are easy to make and will surely make your day:

5.1 Indian Bread Malpua Recipe

Preparation Time: 30 minutes
Cooking Time: 20 minutes
Serving: 4

Ingredients:

- Cardamom powder, one teaspoon
- Khoya, half cup
- Saffron thread, a quarter teaspoon
- Unsalted butter, one tablespoon
- Chopped cashews, two tablespoon
- Raisins, two tablespoon
- Milk, one cup
- Chopped pistachios, two tablespoon
- Sugar, two cups
- Grated coconut, half cup

Instructions:
1. Add the sugar in same quantity of water.
2. Boil the water to make sure the sugar dissolves.
3. Add the rest of the ingredients into a bowl.
4. Mix all the things well and then form small balls.

5. Fry the balls and then add them to the sugary water.
6. Cook them for ten minutes.
7. Your dish is ready to be served.

5.2 Indian Gulab Jamun Recipe

Preparation Time: 30 minutes
Cooking Time: 20 minutes
Serving: 4

Ingredients:

- Cardamom powder, one teaspoon
- Milk powder, two cup
- Unsalted butter, one tablespoon
- Chopped badaam, two tablespoon
- Sooji, half cup
- Egg, two
- Chopped pistachios, two tablespoon
- Sugar, two cups
- Grated coconut, half cup

Instructions:
1. Take equal quantity of sugar and water i.e. two cups of sugar and two cups of water.
2. Add the sugar in same quantity of water.
3. Boil the water to make sure the sugar dissolves.
4. Add the rest of the ingredients into a bowl.
5. Mix all the things well and then form small balls.
6. Fry the balls and then add them to the sugary water.
7. Cook them for ten minutes.
8. Dish out the gulab jamun.

9. Your dish is ready to be served.

5.3 Indian Instant Pot Coconut Rice Kheer Recipe

Preparation Time: 20 minutes
Cooking Time: 20 minutes
Serving: 4

Ingredients:

- Pure ghee, two tablespoon
- Condensed milk, two tablespoon
- Sugar, one cup
- Milk, one and half cup
- Rice, two cup
- Raisins, one cup
- Chopped cashew nuts, one cup
- Cardamom powder, one teaspoon

Instructions:
1. Take an instant pot.
2. Add the pure ghee into it.
3. Add the rice into the ghee.
4. Fry the rice for about five minutes.
5. Add the sugar into the mixture and melt the sugar.
6. Add the milk and rest of the ingredients into the mixture.
7. Close the lid of the instant pot and let the kheer cook for about five minutes.
8. The dish is ready to be served.

5.4 Indian Bread Pudding Recipe

Preparation Time: 30 minutes
Cooking Time: 10 minutes
Serving: 4

Ingredients:

- Chopped bread, one bowl
- Butter, one cup
- Eggs, two
- All-purpose flour, two cups
- Water, as required
- Baking soda, one tablespoon
- Salt, a pinch
- Whipped cream, one cup
- Cornstarch, half cup

Instructions:
1. Take a large bowl and clean it well.
2. Add the sugar and baking soda.
3. Add the salt and cream.
4. Mix all the ingredients well.
5. Add the beaten eggs into the mixture.
6. Add the bread pieces into it.
7. Boil the whole mixture for ten minutes.
8. Cool it down in a large bowl.
9. Refrigerate it for fifty minutes.
10. Add the whipped cream on top of the pudding.
11. The dish is ready to be served.

5.5 Indian Carrot Halwa Recipe

Preparation Time: 20 minutes
Cooking Time: 40 minutes
Serving: 4

Ingredients:

- Pure ghee, two tablespoon
- Condensed milk, two tablespoon
- Milk, half cup
- Sugar, one cup
- Khoya, one and half cup
- Shredded carrot, two cup
- Raisins, one cup
- Water, half cup
- Chopped cashew nuts, one cup
- Cardamom powder, one teaspoon

Instructions:
1. Take a large pan.
2. Add the shredded carrots and milk into it and cook them for twenty minutes until the milk dries.
3. Add pure ghee into another pan.
4. Add the cooked carrots into the ghee.
5. Fry the carrots for about five minutes.
6. Add the sugar into the mixture and melt the sugar.
7. Add the khoya, condensed milk and rest of the ingredients into the mixture.
8. Cook the halwa for about fifteen to twenty minutes.
9. The dish is ready to be served.

5.6 Indian Rava Kessari Recipe

Preparation Time: 20 minutes
Cooking Time: 20 minutes
Serving: 4

Ingredients:

- Pure ghee, two tablespoon
- Kessari color, two tablespoon
- Sugar, one cup
- Rava, one and half cup
- Water, two cup
- Raisins, one cup
- Sooji, one cup
- Chopped cashew nuts, one cup
- Cardamom powder, one teaspoon

Instructions:
1. Take a large pan.
2. Add the pure ghee into it.
3. Add the rava and sooji into the ghee.
4. Fry the ingredients for about five minutes.
5. Add the sugar into the mixture and melt the sugar.
6. Add the water and rest of the ingredients into the mixture.
7. Cook the kessari for about fifteen to twenty minutes.
8. The dish is ready to be served.

5.7 Indian Coconut Laddu Recipe

Preparation Time: 20 minutes
Cooking Time: 60 minutes
Serving: 4

Ingredients:

- Pure ghee, two tablespoon
- Sugar, one cup
- Milk, half cup
- Desiccated coconut, one cup
- Chopped almonds, one cup
- Cardamom powder, one teaspoon

Instructions:
1. Take a large pan.
2. Add the pure ghee and desiccated coconut into it.
3. Cook the coconut for about five minutes.
4. Add the sugar into the mixture and melt the sugar.
5. Add the milk and rest of the ingredients into the mixture.
6. Cook the mixture until it turns thick in consistency.
7. Dish it out and make small balls.
8. The dish is ready to be served.

5.8 Indian Basundi Recipe

Preparation Time: 30 minutes
Cooking Time: 10 minutes
Serving: 4

Ingredients:

- Milk, two cups
- Condensed milk, three cups
- Cardamom powder, one teaspoon
- Nutmeg powder, a pinch
- Saffron threads, one teaspoon
- Mixed nuts, one cup

Instructions:
1. Add the liquid ingredients in a blender.
2. Blend the ingredients together.
3. Add the rest of the ingredients into the liquid mixture.
4. Pour the mixture into glasses.
5. Your dish is ready to be served.

5.9 Indian Mango Shirkhand Recipe

Preparation Time: 30 minutes
Cooking Time: 10 minutes
Serving: 4

Ingredients:

- Curd, two cups
- Chopped mangoes, three cups
- Cardamom powder, one teaspoon
- Sugar, half cup
- Saffron threads, one teaspoon
- Mixed nuts, one cup

Instructions:
1. Add the mango, sugar and curd in a blender.
2. Blend the ingredients together.
3. Add the rest of the ingredients into the liquid mixture.
4. Pour the mixture into glasses.
5. Your dish is ready to be served.

5.10 Indian Moong Daal Halwa Recipe

Preparation Time: 20 minutes
Cooking Time: 20 minutes
Serving: 4

Ingredients:

- Pure ghee, two tablespoon
- Condensed milk, two tablespoon
- Sugar, one cup
- Khoya, one and half cup
- Moong daal, two cup
- Raisins, one cup
- Water, half cup
- Chopped cashew nuts, one cup
- Cardamom powder, one teaspoon

Instructions:
1. Take a large pan.
2. Add the pure ghee into it.
3. Add the moong daal into the ghee.
4. Fry the daal for about five minutes.
5. Add the sugar into the mixture and melt the sugar.
6. Add the khoya and rest of the ingredients into the mixture.
7. Cook the halwa for about fifteen to twenty minutes.
8. The dish is ready to be served.

Chapter 6: Authentic Indian Recipes Eaten Only by Indian People

There are varieties of recipes that are only eaten by Indians around the world. Following are some of the recipes:

6.1 Indian Vada Pav Recipe

Preparation Time: 40 minutes
Cooking Time: 20 minutes
Serving: 4

Ingredients:

- Oil, two teaspoon
- Garlic cloves, two
- Kashmiri red chili, two teaspoon
- Salt, to taste
- Cilantro, one bunch
- Green chilies, one
- Cumin powder, one teaspoon
- Lime juice, one teaspoon
- Water, as needed
- Tamarind paste, half cup
- Jaggery, few grams
- Ginger powder, one teaspoon
- Mustard seeds, one teaspoon
- Hing, half teaspoon
- Turmeric, half teaspoon
- Chopped cilantro, two tablespoon
- Potatoes, two
- Besan, one cup
- Baking soda, a pinch

- Ladi pav, ten
- Butter, as needed

Instructions:
1. Heat the oil in a pan.
2. Add the garlic and fry it until it becomes brown in color.
3. Add the coconut and cook it well.
4. Add the toasted garlic and coconut to a blender.
5. Add the salt, red chili powder and pepper if needed.
6. You have the garlic chutney.
7. To prepare green chutney, add the cilantro, green chili, garlic, cumin, salt and lime juice in a blender and blend all ingredients to form a paste.
8. To make tamarind chutney, add the water in a pan.
9. Add the tamarind paste, jaggery, salt, red chili powder, cumin powder, ginger powder and pepper in the pan.
10. Boil all the ingredients to have a paste type material.
11. Heat the oil in a pan and add the mustard seeds, curry leaves, ginger, garlic, boiled potatoes, turmeric, green chili, chopped cilantro and lemons.
12. Cook the ingredients well and mash them well.
13. Make round balls out of this potato mixture.
14. To make batter, take basin in a bowl and add turmeric, baking soda, water and salt to it.
15. Heat the oil in a wok and dip each of the potato rounds into the batter and coat it.

16. Fry the vada until they become golden brown.
17. Your dish is ready to be served with the variety of chutney already prepared.

6.2 Indian Dhokla Recipe

Preparation Time: 30 minutes
Cooking Time: 10 minutes
Serving: 4

Ingredients:

- Gram flour, one cup
- Semolina, one teaspoon
- Oil, one tablespoon
- Water, one cup
- Salt, to taste
- Pepper, to taste
- Green chili, one
- Lemon juice, one teaspoon

Instructions:
1. Heat the water and take it out in a bowl.
2. Add the gram flour, semolina, lemon juice, green chili, salt and pepper in the bowl.
3. Mix all ingredients to make a smooth batter.
4. Pour the batter over greased plates.
5. Place the plates in steamer and steam it for ten minutes.
6. Your dish is ready to be served.

6.3 Indian Masala Dosa Recipe

Preparation Time: 10 minutes
Cooking Time: 50 minutes
Serving: 4

Ingredients:

- Rice, one cup
- Urad dal, half cup
- Vegetable oil, for frying
- Ginger powder, one teaspoon
- Garlic cloves, two
- Cumin seeds, one teaspoon
- Curry leaves, one
- Mustard seeds, one teaspoon
- Sesame seeds, one teaspoon
- Chopped coriander leaves, two tablespoon
- Fresh coconut, one tablespoon
- Hing, a pinch

Instructions:
1. Make dosa batter by adding rice in bowl with water.
2. Add the Urad dal and rinse well.
3. Put the rice in blender and make a smooth paste.
4. Combine both pastes.
5. Add the oil in a skillet and heat it.
6. Add the cumin seeds, mustard seeds and coriander leaves.
7. Add the garlic, ginger, green chili, salt and pepper.
8. Add turmeric, onion, potato, and water to it.
9. Mash them all well.

10. Heat the oil in separate skillet.
11. Spread the dosa batter over it in circles.
12. In the end add the potato mixture over top of dosa.
13. Your dish is ready to be served.

6.4 Indian Babinka Recipe

Preparation Time: 10 minutes
Cooking Time: 50 minutes
Serving: 4

Ingredients:

- Eggs, two
- Sugar, to taste
- Coconut milk, half cup
- Butter, half cup
- Gram flour, half cup
- Nutmeg powder, few grams

Instructions:
1. Take a bowl and mix coconut milk, flour, sugar, nutmeg, eggs and some water to have a batter.
2. Bake the batter until it turns golden brown.
3. Your dish is ready to be served.

6.5 Indian Bamboo Steam Fish Recipe

Preparation Time: 5 minutes
Cooking Time: 50 minutes
Serving: 4

> **Ingredients:**
>
> - Fish, one pound
> - Bamboo shoots, few inches' long
> - Indian spices, as needed
> - Leaves, as needed

Instructions:
1. Take the bamboo shoots and chop them.
2. Add the fish to it.
3. Add all the spices.
4. Steam the fish over coal flames.
5. Your dish is ready to be served.

6.6 Indian Kondi Kura Recipe

Preparation Time: 10 minutes
Cooking Time: 40 minutes
Serving: 4

> **Ingredients:**
>
> - Chicken, one pound
> - Onions, two
> - Garam masala, one teaspoon
> - Water, one cup
> - Vegetable oil, for frying
> - Ginger powder, one teaspoon

- Garlic cloves, two
- Cumin seeds, one teaspoon
- Curry leaves, one
- Mustard seeds, one teaspoon
- Sesame seeds, one teaspoon
- Chopped coriander leaves, two tablespoon
- Sesame oil, one tablespoon

Instructions:
1. Dry roast the coriander seeds, mustard seeds, cumin seeds, ginger, garlic, chili powder, salt and pepper.
2. In a mortar, grind all the ingredients.
3. Take pressure cooker and add the chicken pieces to it.
4. Add the turmeric, onions, garam masala and curry leaves.
5. Add the ground material.
6. Cook well.
7. Your dish is ready to be served.

6.7 Indian Bhuttay ke Kheer Recipe

Preparation Time: 20 minutes
Cooking Time: 20 minutes
Serving: 4

Ingredients:

- Pure ghee, two tablespoon
- Condensed milk, two tablespoon
- Sugar, one cup
- Milk, one and half cup
- Corn, two cup

- Raisins, one cup
- Chopped cashew nuts, one cup
- Cardamom powder, one teaspoon

Instructions:
1. Take a large pan.
2. Add the pure ghee into it.
3. Add the boiled corn into the ghee.
4. Fry the corn for about five minutes.
5. Add the sugar into the mixture and melt the sugar.
6. Add the milk and rest of the ingredients into the mixture.
7. Cook the kheer for about fifteen to twenty minutes.
8. The dish is ready to be served.

6.8 Indian Sidu Recipe

Preparation Time: 30 minutes
Cooking Time: 25 minutes
Serving: 4

Ingredients:

- Pastry sheets, as required
- Cooking oil, for frying
- Egg wash, one

For the filling:
- Paneer, half cup
- Roasted peanuts, half cup
- Cooked peas, one cup
- Garlic and ginger paste, one

> teaspoon
> - Walnuts, one teaspoon

Instructions:
1. In a large bowl, make the filling by mixing all the ingredients.
2. Roll the pastry sheets.
3. Add a little filling.
4. Fold the pastry slices into a sandwich.
5. Fold them with milk and egg wash.
6. Add oil into a large pan.
7. Heat it and add the sandwich pieces.
8. Fry the sandwiches until they turn golden brown from all sides.
9. Your dish is ready to be served.

6.9 Indian Tabak Maax Recipe

Preparation Time: 10 minutes
Cooking Time: 10 minutes
Serving: 4

> **Ingredients:**
>
> - Dried ginger powder, two teaspoon
> - Milk, one cup
> - Cinnamon powder, one teaspoon
> - Lamb ribs, one pound
> - Aniseed powder, half teaspoon
> - Ghee, half cup
> - Turmeric powder, one teaspoon
> - Minced garlic, two tablespoon

Instructions:
1. Take a large pan.
2. Add the ghee and garlic paste into the pan.
3. Cook them well and then add the rest of the ingredients.
4. Place a lid on the pan and reduce the heat.
5. Cook the ingredients for twenty minutes.
6. Your dish is ready to be served.

6.10 Indian Sarson ka Saag Recipe

Preparation Time: 20 minutes
Cooking Time: 120 minutes
Serving: 4

Ingredients:

- Mustard leaves, one bunch
- Fenugreek leaves, one bunch
- Radish leaves, one bunch
- Chopped tomatoes, one cup
- Fresh ginger, one teaspoon
- Chopped onion, one cup
- Red chili powder, one tablespoon
- Fresh shiso leaves, two tablespoon
- Water, three cups
- Maize flour, one tablespoon
- Green chilies, one teaspoon
- Ghee, half cup

Instructions:
1. Heat a large pan.
2. Add the ghee and let it heat.
3. Add the onions and garlic.

4. Add the rest of the ingredients.
5. Let the ingredients cook for about two hours straight on a low heat.
6. Your dish is ready to be served.

Conclusion

In every country of the world, you will definitely find an Indian eatery or a café that offers Indian food. Indian cooking has a great impact with regards to the special taste of food. Many societies in the world additionally try to cook this wonderful cuisine at home. It is by far one of the most famous cuisines ever.

After reading this book, you will realize that making your favorite Indian food at home is not difficult at all. This cookbook includes 70 recipes that contain breakfast, lunch, dinner, dessert and authentic recipes eaten by only Indian people. You can easily make these recipes at home without supervision of any kind. So, start cooking today and enjoy cooking your delicious Indian food at home.

INDIAN
COOKBOOK

70 Easy Recipes for Traditional Food from India

Maki Blanc

© Copyright 2021 by Maki Blanc - All rights reserved.

This document is geared towards providing exact and reliable information in regard to the topic and issue covered. The publication is sold with the idea that the publisher is not required to render accounting, officially permitted, or otherwise, qualified services. If advice is necessary, legal or professional, a practiced individual in the profession should be ordered.

- From a Declaration of Principles which was accepted and approved equally by a Committee of the American Bar Association and a Committee of Publishers and Associations.

It is not legal in any way to reproduce, duplicate, or transmit any part of this document in either electronic means or in printed format. Recording of this publication is strictly prohibited and any storage of this document is not allowed unless with written permission from the publisher. All rights reserved.

The information provided herein is stated to be truthful and consistent, in that any liability, in terms of inattention or otherwise, by any usage or abuse of any policies, processes, or directions contained within is the solitary and utter responsibility of the recipient reader. Under no circumstances will any legal responsibility or blame be held against the publisher for any reparation, damages, or monetary loss due to the information herein, either directly or indirectly.

Respective authors own all copyrights not held by the publisher.

The information herein is offered for informational purposes solely and is universal as so. The presentation of the information is without contract or any type of guarantee assurance.

The trademarks that are used are without any consent, and the publication of the trademark is without permission or backing by the trademark owner. All trademarks and brands within this book are for clarifying purposes only and are the owned by the owners themselves, not affiliated with this document.

Contents

INTRODUCTION 120

CHAPTER 1: INTRODUCTION TO INDIAN CUISINE 122

1.1 History of Indian Cuisine 123

1.2 History of Traditional Dishes of Indian Food 124

1.3 Nutritional Information and Benefits of Indian Food 124

1.4 Key ingredients of Indian Food 126

CHAPTER 2: INDIAN APPETIZERS RECIPES 127

2.1 Nippattu 127

2.2 Thattai 128

2.3 Shankarpali 129

2.4 Namak Para 130

2.5 Jhal Muri 131

2.6 Spring Rolls 133

2.7 Punugulu 134

2.8 Vegetable Cutlets 135

CHAPTER 3: INDIAN BREAKFAST RECIPES 137

3.1 Soft Idli 137

3.2 Crispy Dosa 138

3.3 Uttapam 140

3.4 Pesarattu 141

3.5 Egg Toast 142

3.6 Egg Paratha 143

3.7 Egg Mayo Sandwich 144

CHAPTER 4: INDIAN SNACK RECIPES 145

4.1 Vegetable Pakora 145

4.2 Onion Pakoras 146

4.3 Mysore Bonda 148

4.4 Churumuri 149

4.5 Crispy Corn 150

4.6 Chakli 151

4.7 Dahi Vada 152

4.8 Dahi Kebab 154

CHAPTER 5: INDIAN LUNCH RECIPES 155

5.1 Cauliflower Korma 155

5.2 Chicken Madras Curry 156

5.3 Ennai Kathirikai Kulambu 158

5.4 Chana Dal 159

5.5 Mughlai Biryani 161

5.6 Veg Pulao 163

5.7 Brinjal Rice 164

5.8 Drumstick Sambar 166

5.9 Navratan Korma 168

CHAPTER 6: INDIAN DINNER RECIPES 170

6.1 Mushroom Biryani 170

6.2 Bisi Bele Bath 171

6.3 Paneer Butter Masala 173

6.4 Vangi Bath 174

6.5 Kashmiri Pulao 176

6.6 Porsha Kuzhambu 177

6.7 Potato Kurma 178

6.8 Matar Paneer 180

CHAPTER 7: INDIAN DESSERTS RECIPES 181

7.1 Besan Lado Recipe 181

7.2 Ras Malai Recipe 182

7.3 Kaju Katli Recipe 183

7.4 Boondi Lado Recipe 184

7.5 Kheer Recipe 185

7.6 Falooda Recipe 186

7.7 Fruit Custard Recipe 187

CHAPTER 8: INDIAN SOUPS DISHES 188

8.1 Cream of Mushroom Soup 188

8.2 Tomato Soup Recipe 189

8.3 Palak Soup 190

8.4 Easy One-Pot Corn Soup 191

8.5 Creamy Bottle Gourd Soup 192

8.6 Roasted Tomato Soup 193

8.7 Carrot Tomato Soup 194

8.8 Cream of Broccoli Soup 195

CHAPTER 9: INDIAN SALAD RECIPES 197

9.1 Bean Sprouts and Salad Recipe 197

9.2 Broccoli and Baby Corn Salad 198

9.3 Rajma Salad 199

9.4 Paneer and Chana Salad 199

9.5 Healthy Lunch Salad 200

9.6 Bean Sprout and Macaroni Salad 202

9.7 Peas and Potato Salad 203

9.8 Cabbage and Grape Salad 204

CHAPTER 10: MOST FAMOUS INDIAN DISHES 206

10.1 Rajma Chawal 206

10.2 Lucknowi Biryani 207

10.3 Chana Masala 209

10.4 Kadhi Chawal 210

10.5 Masala Dosa 212

10.6 Dal Makhani 214

10.7 Rogan Josh..215

CONCLUSION..**218**

Introduction

Seasoning blends, heady herbs, and bright colors prevail in Indian cuisine, aromatic and tasty. It also contains anti-inflammatory micronutrients in abundance. If Indian cuisine is unfamiliar to you, it can seem intimidating, but do not worry: these dishes describe in the book are surprisingly simple to prepare. Indeed, once you have had a few culinary triumphs, you might choose to create Indian-influenced dishes, a frequent part of your culinary range. Fragrant spices, which are a staple of Indian cuisine, are better when used fresh. You will save money by purchasing fresh spices in limited amounts from your nearest natural foods market's bulk section.

In terms of cuisine, India can be split into four distinct regions. Each area contains numerous nations, each with its distinct cuisine. Here is a quick rundown of North, East, South, and West Indian delicacies. Of course, it is important to keep in mind that no single explanation can encompass the vast array of Indian cuisine. It can take years of meticulous and really enjoyable gastronomic exploration to discover it.

Indian cuisine offers a wide variety of flavors, both strong and subtle, that is as diverse as the country itself. Weather and elevation, as well as culture and faith, both have an impact on the area. They describe a broad range of cuisines, which is unsurprising in a world with an estimated 885 million people and a land area of 1,226,596 square miles. Aside from herbs' prominent use, flatbreads and much larger milk products than anywhere in Asia are traditional culinary threads that run through local cuisines. Based on the region, baked goods are made from wheat, rice, or ground vegetables, while processed foods include milk, cream, yogurt, heavy cream, cream cheese, and cheese.

Religion has unquestionably had the greatest impact on Indian cuisine. Centuries of Hindu tradition and a deep conviction in reincarnation have culminated in some of the world's most delectable vegetarian food. Vegans rely on a variety of whole and split vegetables for nutrition. They have a wholesome, diverse diet combined with grain, supported by vegetables and milk products, and flavored to the full. Indian cuisine is similar to defining European cuisine in that it encompasses all at once.

"Indian Cookbook" is a complete recipe book based on all types of Indian dishes. It has four chapters with detailed knowledge of the introduction to Indian cuisine. Recipes from different regions of India are given in each chapter. These chapters are characterized into breakfast, appetizers, snacks, lunch, dinner, desserts, soups, salad, and India's most famous dishes. Try these dishes at your home and make your meals more like Indians.

Chapter 1: Introduction to Indian Cuisine

Food and drink are considered to nourish both the soul and the skin in India; food is central to spiritual development, pleasure, and happiness. The Indian kitchen differs greatly from north to eastern side to south, with western and southern Indian curries leading the way to vegan Indian food since most Western people recognize and enjoy it.

A cook's ingenuity and situations are the only limits to the richness of Indian cuisine. Each Indian chef, rest assured, would be a master of seasoning, handling each one separately before mixing them into different masalas (spice blends). Indians, like foreigners, are passionate about their cuisine. Three meals per day are normal, but certain areas of the country are so impoverished that they can only manage one. More than 500 million Indians, out of a total population of 1.2 billion, survive on less than $2.50 per day. However, whoever can enjoy their three primary meals and pack as many tiffins (snack foods) as they can into their everyday diet without sabotaging their hunger.

1.1 History of Indian Cuisine

Ayurveda, the ancient philosophy of life, fitness, and immortality, has influenced modern Indian culinary traditions. Foods are classified in Ayurveda based on their positive and negative forces and medicinal benefits. It is now the most commonly practiced treatment system in India, established by the Aryans in the second millennium BC. The fundamental theory of 'you are what you consume – you consume accordingly to what you are' is that you cannot sustain a balanced body by eating inappropriate food.

Much of this has not prevented fast-food franchises from establishing themselves in India's megacities like Mumbai, Delhi, and Calcutta. However, the ordinary Indian will still choose home-cooked food and a nearby ayurvedic practitioner to everything else. Moreover, although meat (except beef) is not specifically forbidden in Hinduism, a number of Indians are vegetarians due to the close connection between moral purity and veganism. Ahimsa (non-injury) is a Hindu and Jains ideology, but Buddhism has a much less humane perspective and is more concerned with intellectual development than animal health.

Such foods are considered pure and holy, and they can be used in temple rituals. The Hindu pantheon has a favorite dish; Krishna, for example, enjoys dairy goods, while Ganesha is often represented with a bowl of modak. Prasad is any meal that is first given to the deities and then exchanged with others.

1.2 History of Traditional Dishes of Indian Food

Indians are voracious consumers of home-cooked food or something done in the privacy of their own homes. The idea of dining in cafes and a posh Indian restaurant tradition has only been around for around fifty years. The Indian side of the road restaurants known as Dhaba is more like a lifestyle – an oasis for truckers, bus riders, and tourists going anywhere by the highway in India's vast, scenic, and often demanding landscape are as common as residence food. India's traditional dishes have roots in the Muslim-Indian era.

Indians are passionate about their food. Cooking is regarded as an art form, and moms often begin teaching their girls and passing down traditional foods by show-and-tell when their daughters are young. Mealtimes are significant moments for family gatherings. The majority of meals consist of many dishes ranging from basics such as rice and bread to meat and veg, followed by a dessert. Food is prepared from home with quality ingredients in many Indian families. Instead of buying grain from a supermarket, some families buy their favorite kind of grain, wash it, drying it in the heat, and then bring it to a factory to have it processed into flour just the way they like it! This is happening in larger cities, where people are happier to use ready-to-eat, pre-made foods because their lives are becoming more hectic.

1.3 Nutritional Information and Benefits of Indian Food

There are many benefits of Indian cuisine.
Chickpeas, for instance, which are frequently used in vegan curries, are high in fiber, calcium, riboflavin, and phosphorus, making them a nutritious addition to a vegan Indian diet. Superfoods such as broccoli and carrots, commonly used in Indian cuisine, produce rich antioxidants, nutrients, and minerals. Most Indian sauces and toppings, like Sag aloo and Gobhi Aloo (cabbage with vegetables), are veggies, making them a healthier option because they do not use milk or dairy. The tangy yogurt dipping raita, made with natural milk, tomato, and mint, is a low-fat option to sauces like mayonnaise and is a source of nutrients. In place of milk or cocoa powder, natural porridge is sometimes used to make curry preserves.

Garlic, which would be good for health, and cloves, which are great for the immune response and digestion, are commonly used in Indian cuisine. Instead of butter, Indian dishes frequently use grain, red pepper, and rice flour, maintaining the saturated fat content. Finally, since Indian dishes have such a strong flavor, a limited portion may also please taste buds while consuming fewer calories. The versatility and vibrancy of an Indian diet make it exciting, which is a good aspect of any cuisine because variety prevents repetition and overeating.

Finally, choosing tandoori recipes will reduce fat and calorie intake since they have very few sauces, and the meal, which is usually poultry and seafood, is grilled rather than fried.

Mango, bananas, pomegranates, figs, tomatoes, strawberries, grapefruit, oranges, and guavas are among the many delights of an Indian diet be consumed regularly to aid digestion and acquire minerals and vitamins.

1.4 Key ingredients of Indian Food

Here are some of the most important spices in Indian cooking.

Garam Masala: Garam means "hot" or "warm" in Hindi, and this mix of chilly spices from northwestern India's cooler climates brings a sense of heat both to the mouth and the soul.

Fenugreek: This herbal tree is found for its surprisingly bitter, somewhat sweet leaves, rich and round with a mild crunch.

Cinnamon's flavor and scent are distinctively woody, stinky, and velvety, and it has a warming effect on the palate.

Coconuts: Coconut milk and oils are essential in Northern Indian cooking, commonly used in curries.

Cumin has a distinct musty, earthy taste with some yellowish notes, making it an essential component in garam masala and chili powder.
Mint: This calming herb has a surprisingly fresh, herbal, sweet taste that goes well with lamb recipes and is used in raitas and curries.
Cardamom is a spice that is used in cooking. Cardamom has a lime, herbal, soapy taste with some bright yellow notes, making it an essential spice in garam masala.
Turmeric is a dried powdered root with a musky, oaky scent and a peppery, mildly bitter taste.
Chiles are native to South America and were brought to India by the Dutch.
Tamarind: Also known as Indian date, condensed tamarind paste is used to give curries and sauces a sour taste.
Cloves have a heavy, pungent, soft, almost spicy taste.
Cilantro: Cilantro (clean cilantro) has a waxy, citrusy, and soapy taste and fragrance.

Chapter 2: Indian Appetizers Recipes

2.1 Nippattu

Cooking Time: 30 minutes
Serving Size: 15-20
Ingredients:
- ¼ cup water or less
- Oil for frying
- ¾ teaspoon salt or as required
- 2 tablespoon hot oil
- 2 sprigs curry leaves
- 1 teaspoon red chili powder
- 1 cup rice flour
- 2 tablespoon dry coconut
- 1 tablespoon sesame seeds
- 2 tablespoon all-purpose flour
- ¼ cup peanuts
- 3 tablespoon fried gram
- 2 tablespoon chiroti rava

Method:
1. Dry roast groundnuts in a skillet until the skin begins to peel.
2. Add the dry coconut and bake for 20-30 seconds with the groundnut.
3. In a machine, combine all of the ingredients.
4. Set that aside after pulsing it into a gritty powder.
5. Add rice flour to the same pot and dry bake for two minutes on medium heat.
6. Insert the all-purpose starch and rava, and proceed to roast for 1 minute more.

7. Merge fine groundnut dust, dried chili powder, minced curry leaves, green onions, and salts in this roast rice flour.
8. Add the oil for frying over medium-high heat.
9. Pick the rolled pastry and gently place it in the hot oil.
10. Take the fried nippattu out of the oil and serve.

2.2 Thattai

Cooking Time: 40 minutes
Serving Size: 25 thattai

Ingredients:
For Roasting
- 1 cup rice flour
- 1 tablespoon urad dal

Other Ingredients
- 10 tablespoons water
- Oil as required
- ½ teaspoon red chili powder
- 2 tablespoons coconut
- ½ teaspoon salt
- 1 teaspoon white sesame seeds
- 1 tablespoon chana dal
- ¼ teaspoon asafoetida powder
- 1 tablespoon chana dal
- 1 tablespoon curry leaves
- 1 tablespoon butter

Method:
1. Wash the chana dal and keep it in hot water for a few minutes.
2. A hardpan should be heated. Toss in the urad dal.
3. For 2 minutes, gently roast the urad dal.
4. Add rice flour to the same plate.

5. Fry the corn starch on moderate to medium heat, often moving, until it is soft to the touch.
6. Keep the roasted urad dal and grind it in a small mixer.
7. Add roasted chana dal as well.
8. Combine the rest of the ingredients, as well as the spices.
9. Mix the butter and flour with your fingertips.
10. To make a semi-soft dough, combine all ingredients and knead until smooth.
11. In a skillet, keep oil for slow cooking.
12. Shape the dough into little balls.
13. Put softly in the hot oil.
14. Start frying the thattai on medium heat.
15. Fry the thattai until it is crisp and golden brown.

2.3 Shankarpali

Cooking Time: 1 hour
Serving Size: 1 jar

Ingredients:
- 3 to 3.5 tablespoon milk
- 2 tablespoon ghee
- ½ cup regular sugar
- 1 pinch salt
- ½ cup Rava
- 1.5 cups all-purpose flour

Method:
1. In a dry mixer, dust the sugar and set it aside.
2. To begin, salt the flour and sieve it.
3. The crushed sugar should then be sieved.
4. The oil should be warm.
5. Make a breadcrumb-like texture by mixing the fat into the flour mix.

6. Heat the milk in the microwave.
7. Then, one tablespoon at a time, insert the hot milk and whisk to a strong, tight mixture.
8. Cover and set aside for thirty minutes.
9. In a skillet, heat the oil for slow cooking.
10. Divide the dough into two parts is a good idea.
11. Transfer 8 of these cuts into the pan softly.
12. If you have a larger skillet, you can cook more.
13. Fry the shankarpali until golden brown.
14. Create diamond-shaped pieces out of the other slice of dough in the same way.
15. Fry such cuts too in quantities and serve.

2.4 Namak Para

Cooking Time: 1 hour 5 minutes
Serving Size: 4

Ingredients:
- Salt to taste
- Oil for frying
- 2 to 3 tablespoon oil
- ½ to ¾ cup water
- 1 teaspoon cumin seeds
- ¼ teaspoon baking soda
- 1 teaspoon carom seeds
- 1 teaspoon black pepper
- 1 cup all-purpose flour
- 1 cup wheat flour

Method:
1. Combine the whole wheat grain, wheat bread, white vinegar, and salt in a large mixing bowl.

2. Carom seeds can be included now.
3. Combine the carom seeds and the remaining sieved flours.
4. Start kneading the dough with the water.
5. Shape the dough into medium-sized spheres and roll them in flour.
6. Create criss-cross shapes on the rolling dough with a sharp blade.
7. Take the diamond-shaped designs from the skillet and pan-fry them in hot oil until lightly browned and crispy.
8. When they have cooled down, place them in an airtight container.
9. Namak para can be served with tea or as a snack.

2.5 Jhal Muri

Cooking Time: 15 minutes
Serving Size: 3

Ingredients:
Main Ingredients
- 1 teaspoon lemon juice
- 2 tablespoons coconut
- 1 teaspoon mustard oil
- 3 tablespoons coriander leaves
- 2 cups puffed rice
- ¼ cup roasted peanuts
- 3 tablespoons chana chur
- ¼ cup onions
- 1 to 2 green chilies
- ½ teaspoon ginger
- ¼ cup tomato
- ½ cup boiled potatoes
- ¼ cup cucumber

Spice Powders
- ½ teaspoon black salt

- ½ teaspoon rock salt
- ¼ teaspoon garam masala powder
- 1 teaspoon mango powder
- ½ teaspoon coriander powder
- ¼ teaspoon black pepper
- ½ teaspoon red chili powder
- ½ teaspoon cumin powder

Method:
1. To begin, finely chop the vegetables.
2. Set them aside for now.
3. Heat a wok over moderate to medium heat.
4. Put two cups of puffed rice into the mixture.
5. Turn off the heat and place the pan on the counter.
6. The fire from the skillet will roast and aromatize the spice powders.
7. Combine the puffed rice and seasoning powders in a mixing bowl.
8. Add ¼ cup roasted peanuts to the mix.
9. The coarsely diced onions, peppers, mushrooms, diced peppers, and ginger are then added.
10. After that, squirt one teaspoon of lime juice all over.
11. Re-blend gently.
12. Add sev to the mixture. You may also use chana chur rather than sev.
13. Coriander leaf should be added at this stage.
14. Taste and season with more salt, lime juice, or seasoning powders if desired.
15. Jhal muri should be served right away.

2.6 Spring Rolls

Cooking Time: 1 hour
Serving Size: 3

Ingredients:
Filling
- 1½ tablespoon oyster sauce
- 2 teaspoon soy sauce
- 1½ cups green cabbage
- 1 teaspoon cornflour
- 1½ cups carrot
- 1½ cups bean sprouts
- 1 tablespoon oil
- 400g pork
- 6 shiitake mushrooms
- 2 garlic cloves

Spring Rolls
- 1 tablespoon water
- Oil for frying
- 2 teaspoon cornflour
- 20 spring roll wrappers

Sweet and Sour Sauce
- 2 tablespoon tomato ketchup
- 2 teaspoon soy sauce
- ½ cup apple cider vinegar
- 1/3 cup brown sugar
- 2 tablespoon water
- 2 teaspoon cornflour

Method:
1. In a pan or wok, melt the oil over medium temperature.

2. Insert the garlic and whisk rapidly before adding the bacon.
3. Carrots, bean sprouts, lettuce, and mushrooms are all good additions.
4. Cook for three minutes until it has ripened veggies.
5. Cook for two minutes, or until the liquid has evaporated, adding cornflour, sesame oil, and oyster sauce as needed.
6. In a small bowl, combine cornstarch and water.
7. Fill a skillet or big saucepan halfway with oil to twice the height of the spring rolls.
8. Heat on high for a few minutes before hot.
9. Put spring rolls in the oils and fry, turning regularly, for two minutes, or until deep yellow. Repeat for the rest of the spring rolls.
10. Offer with Sweet and Tamarind Chutney while it is still hot!

2.7 Punugulu

Cooking Time: 30 minutes
Serving Size: 2-3

Ingredients:
- Salt as required
- Oil for deep frying
- 3 teaspoon coriander leaves
- 1 teaspoon cumin seeds
- ½ inch ginger
- 1 or 2 green chilies
- 1 cup idli batter
- 1 small onion
- 6 curry leaves
- 1 tablespoon rava

Method:
1. In a mixing dish, combine 1 cup idli mixture or dosa mixture.
2. Insert two to three teaspoon cilantro leaves, chopped garlic, Rava, cabbage, chopped cabbage, curry leaf, sliced mustard seeds, garlic, green chilies, two to three teaspoon cardamom leaves.
3. In a wok or skillet, heat the oil for slow cooking.
4. The exterior should be smooth, while the interior should be warm and plush.
5. If the mixture is too thick, a few teaspoons of water should be added.
6. In moderate oil, drop tablespoons of the batter.
7. Turn over until the sides are pale golden, and clear.
8. Fry them in medium-high heat, rotating them a few times to ensure even browning.
9. Punugulu is best served hot or warm with almond or nut chutney.

2.8 Vegetable Cutlets

Cooking Time: 45 minutes
Serving Size: 3

Ingredients:
- ⅓ cup bread crumbs
- 3 tablespoons oil
- 2 tablespoons all-purpose flour
- 3 tablespoons water
- ½ cup boiled carrots
- ½ teaspoon masala powder
- 3 tablespoons bread crumbs
- 1 cup boiled potatoes
- ¼ teaspoon red chili powder
- ½ teaspoon cumin powder
- ½ inch ginger

- ½ cup fresh green peas

Method:
1. In a broiler pan or heat cooker, thoroughly cook the potato, cabbage, and green peas.
2. When the vegetables are cooling, finely chop four to five slices of toast in a mixing bowl or blender to make bread crumbs.
3. Set aside the bread crumbs on a sheet or plate.
4. Slice and cut the carrots and potatoes.
5. Use a spoon or a masher to smash them.
6. Mix with the rest of the ingredients.
7. Add two tablespoon all-purpose starch and three tablespoon liquid in a separate small bowl.
8. Put the cutlet combination on a plate, then.
9. In a skillet, heat two to three tablespoons of oil for deep frying.
10. Then thinly roll the cutlet in breadcrumbs.
11. Remove any leftover bread crumbs before placing them in the medium-hot liquid.
12. Flip a few more times to ensure that all of the vegetables are cooked through.

Chapter 3: Indian Breakfast Recipes

3.1 Soft Idli

Cooking Time: 9 hours 25 minutes
Serving Size: 30 idli

Ingredients:
- 1 teaspoon rock salt
- Oil as required
- ¼ teaspoon fenugreek seeds
- Water
- ½ cup whole urad dal
- ¼ cup thick poha
- 1 cup regular rice

Method:
1. Both normal and preboiled rice should be picked and rinsed.
2. Fill the container halfway with water.
3. Individually soak the urad dal and methi seeds in liquid for five hours.
4. Drain the urad dal that has been soaked.
5. For a few seconds, grind the urad dal, methi seed, and ¼ cup of the allocated water.
6. Then pour in the remaining ¼ cup of water. Grind until the batter is thick and moist.
7. To form a delicious batter, ground the rice in quantities.
8. Grease the idli molds and set them aside.
9. In a slow cooker or hotplate, pour the mixture into the molds and steam the idli.
10. Heat for 15 to 20 minutes, or until the idlis are cooked through.

11.   Offer the hot steaming idli with sambar and mango chutney.

3.2 Crispy Dosa

Cooking Time: 14 hours
Serving Size: 15 dosa

> **Ingredients:**
> **Dosa Batter**
> - 1 teaspoon rock salt
> - Ghee or oil
> - ½ teaspoon methi seeds
> - 3 tablespoons flattened rice
> - 1 tablespoon chana dal
> - 1 tablespoon toor dal
> - ¾ cup idli rice
> - ½ cup urad dal gota
> - ¾ cup Sona masoori rice
>
> **Potato Masala**
> - ½ teaspoon salt
> - Cilantro to garnish
> - 15 curry leaves
> - ½ teaspoon turmeric powder
> - 4 medium potatoes
> - 1 medium onion
> - 1-2 green chilies
> - 6 cashews broken
> - 1 teaspoon ginger
> - 1 tablespoon oil
> - ¼ teaspoon asafoetida
> - 1 teaspoon chana dal
> - ½ teaspoon mustard seeds

Method:
1. Transfer sona masoori grain, toor dal, urad dal gota, and methi seeds, in a big mixing cup.
2. Pour the water from the grain, dals, and poha before blending it in a high-powered blender.
3. Now, pass the mixture to the Instant Pot's steel pan.
4. One teaspoon rock salt can be added to the mixture.
5. Pour the salt into the mixture for two minutes with your hands.
6. In a medium-sized tub, heat one tablespoon of oil.
7. Toss in the chana dal, cashew nuts, and spice, minced.
8. Add the chopped onion, diced peppers, and coriander seeds after that.
9. Cook for about two minutes, or until the vegetables are softened.
10. Add the cinnamon and pepper to the boiling and whipped potatoes.
11. On medium-high fire, heat a cast iron pan.
12. Cut an onion in half, pierce it with a blade, and then drop it in oil.
13. Then begin preparing the dosa. Fill a ladle halfway with batter and dump it into the pan's middle.
14. Drizzle peanut oil or butter all over the dosa, as well as in the middle.
15. Fold in the cooked potato masala.
16. Prepare all of the dosas in the same manner.
17. Serve fried masala dosas immediately with sambar, coriander coconut lime pickle, or tomatillo salsa.

3.3 Uttapam

Cooking Time: 40 minutes
Serving Size: 8

Ingredients:
- 1 teaspoon kosher salt
- ¼ cup water
- 4 cups Idli Batter

Toppings
- ½ cup cilantro
- ¼ cup ghee
- 2 tomatoes
- 2 to 4 green chilies
- 1 medium red onion

Method:
1. To make a pancake-like texture, add salt and sugar to the idli batter.
2. To make a 6-inch croissant, spread around two spoons full of batter.
3. First, on the uttapam, place one tablespoon onions, pepper, ¼ teaspoon green chili, and ½ tablespoon coriander.
4. With a small silicone spoon, gently pick up the uttapam, coming in from the sides and touching the middle, and turn it over.
5. As the onions begin to caramelize, fry the strong part for 1 to 2 minutes.
6. Remove the uttapam and eat with mango pickle or cilantro leaf chutney and paratha, top side up.
7. Repeat for the rest of the batter.

3.4 Pesarattu

Cooking Time: 4 hours 20 minutes
Serving Size: 7

Ingredients:
For Batter
- 1 tablespoon rice flour
- Salt to taste
- 2 tablespoon chana dal
- Water as required
- 1 cup moong dal

Other Ingredients
- 1-inch ginger
- 1 green chili
- Half onion
- Seven teaspoon oil

Method:
1. First, soak chana dal and mong dal for at minimum up to eight hours in a big mixing cup.
2. Drain the water and mix the batter until it is creamy.
3. Place in a big mixing cup.
4. To put additional crispiness, add corn starch.
5. Season with salt to taste.
6. Shake the batter thoroughly until it reaches the strength of the dosa batter.
7. Using a spoon, spill a ladleful of batter onto a frying pan.
8. Place it thinly in a clockwise direction.
9. Over the pessarattu, spread a little coarsely diced onions, jeera, chili - pepper, and oil.
10. Strip the dosa from the ends gradually.
11. And then fold it into a triangle or some other shape you like.
12. Serve pessarattu with warm uppitu, allam sorbet, or mango pickle as a finishing touch.

3.5 Egg Toast

Cooking Time: 1 toast
Serving Size: 30 minutes

Ingredients:
- Salt, to taste
- Pepper, to taste
- 1 egg
- 3 tablespoons shredded cheese
- ½ tablespoon butter
- 1 slice bread

Method:
1. To make a bowl, press it down on the middle of the loaf with a spoon.
2. Spread the butter around the sides of the loaf and crack the egg into the jar.
3. Spread melted cheese along the bread's sides.
4. Season with salt and pepper and cook for fifteen minutes at 400°F.
5. A runny yolk will result after ten minutes, while a firmer yolk will result after fifteen minutes.

3.6 Egg Paratha

Cooking Time: 30 minutes
Serving Size: 2

Ingredients:
- 2 tablespoon coriander leaves
- ½ teaspoon garam masala
- ¼ cup onions
- 1 green chili
- 2 cups whole wheat flour
- 1 tablespoon oil
- 2 eggs
- A pinch of salt

Method:
1. Add flour, pepper, and oils to a measuring bowl, and whisk the combination into a flat dough with 1 cup of water.
2. If the flour seems to be dry, apply a little more liquid. Knead thoroughly.
3. Make four balls out of the dough.
4. Whisk together the eggs, carrots, chili, coriander, curry powder, and salt in a mixing cup. Set aside for now.
5. Put the rolled pastry on a frying pan and bake on both sides for 1-2 minutes.
6. Cook for another minute after adding a little oil to the surface.
7. Create a slit as soon as the edges begin to crisp.
8. More oil should be drizzled on the paratha, and the layer should be softly pressed with the back of the knife.

3.7 Egg Mayo Sandwich

Cooking Time: 35 minutes
Serving Size: 4

Ingredients:
- Salt and pepper to taste
- ¼ teaspoon paprika
- 1 teaspoon yellow mustard
- ¼ cup green onion
- ½ cup mayonnaise
- 8 eggs

Method:
1. In a frying pan, crack the egg and coat it with ice water.
2. Bring the water to a boil and then remove it from the heat.
3. Allow eggs to sit in hot water for 10 - 15 minutes, covered.
4. Take from the hot water, allow to cool before peeling and slicing.
5. In a mixing dish, combine the diced eggs, mayo, vinegar, and spring onions.
6. Season with parmesan, lime, and pepper.
7. Combine all ingredients in a mixing bowl and serve with your choice of bread or crackers.

Chapter 4: Indian Snack Recipes

4.1 Vegetable Pakora

Cooking Time: 20 minutes
Serving Size: 5

Ingredients:
Ketchup Chutney
- ½ teaspoon sugar
- ½ teaspoon salt
- 1 tablespoon water
- ½ tablespoon chaat masala
- ½ cup ketchup

Pakora Batter
- 1 cup luke-warm water
- Sunflower oil
- ½ cup cilantro leaves
- 1 yellow onion
- 2 cups besan
- ½ teaspoon baking powder
- 1 green chili pepper
- ¾ teaspoon sea salt
- 1 tablespoon red pepper flakes

Method:
1. In a mixing dish, combine all of the chutney components.
2. Half-fill an 8-inch cast-iron pan or other heavy-bottom pot with grease.
3. Preheat the oil to 375 degrees Fahrenheit.
4. Combine the besan, dried chili flakes, flour, icing sugar, sliced chili pepper, coriander, and diced onion in a big mixing cup.

5. Slowly drizzle in the water, constantly stirring with a spoon or your fingers.
6. When the oil is hot enough, gently drop a heaping tablespoon of mixture into it.
7. Fry the pakoras until they are a pecan-brown color.
8. Then use a cooling rack over a baking sheet, clean the pakoras.
9. Continue for the remaining hitter.
10. Serve the hot pakoras with the Tomato sauce Chutney straight away.

4.2 Onion Pakoras

Cooking Time: 30 minutes
Serving Size: 4

Ingredients:
- Water as required
- Salt as required
- 1 pinch baking soda
- Oil as required
- 1 teaspoon carom seeds
- 1 pinch asafoetida
- 2 medium onions
- ½ teaspoon garam masala powder
- ¼ teaspoon turmeric powder
- 1 cup gram flour
- 1 tablespoon coriander leaves
- 2 teaspoon green chilies

Method:
1. Finely chop the onions and place them in a blending dish.
2. Add the chopped green chilies as well.
3. Carom seeds, fenugreek seeds, asafoetida, and salt are added to the pan.

4. Combine all of the ingredients thoroughly.
5. Toss in the gram flour.
6. To make a moderate batter, add the appropriate volume of water.
7. With a fork or your hands, thoroughly combine the ingredients.
8. Transfer tablespoons of the flour to the hot oil.
9. Turn the pakoras over with a slotted spoon when they're almost done and begin to fry.
10. Fry them until they are crispy and fluffy.
11. Remove with a slotted spoon and wash on paper towels to extract any extra oil.
12. Slit green peppers are fried in the same oil.
13. Season the green chilies with salt and toss well.

4.3 Mysore Bonda

Cooking Time: 20 minutes
Serving Size: 4
Ingredients:

- 1 cup all-purpose flour
- ½ teaspoon cooking soda
- 1 cup yogurt
- ¼ cup rice flour
- 3 green chilies
- 1 tablespoon coconut pieces
- Salt - to taste
- 1 teaspoon cumin seeds
- 1 teaspoon ginger
- 1 cup water
- Oil - to fry

Method:
1. Combine the curd and the water in a mixing bowl. Let it aside for now.
2. In a mixing cup, combine all-purpose flour, rice flour, sugar, and soda; stir to combine, then apply buttermilk to create a vada batter texture.
3. Now add the cumin, thinly sliced coconut, diced peppers, coarsely diced ginger, and stir well. Set aside for 1 hour.
4. Heat the oil for frying, then cut the dough into small round bondas and place them in the oil to fry on low heat.
5. Once it has become a light golden hue, extract it. Serve with mango pickle on the side.

4.4 Churumuri

Cooking Time: 10 minutes
Serving Size: 2

Ingredients:
- 1 teaspoon lemon juice
- ¼ cup sev

- 1 green chili
- 3 tablespoons coriander leaves
- 2 cups puffed rice
- 1 small carrot
- 2 tablespoons green mango
- ¼ cup peanuts
- 1 small to medium onion
- 1 medium tomato
- 1 teaspoon red chili powder
- ¼ to ⅓ teaspoon salt
- 3 pinches black salt
- 1 tablespoon coconut oil
- 3 pinches turmeric powder

Method:
1. Vegetables should be peeled, rinsed, and finely chopped.
2. In a bowl or skillet, heat ½ tablespoon essential oils.
3. Place the puffed rice on top.
4. Puffed rice grain should be roasted until crisp and chewy.
5. Put the puffed rice in the skillet and wait two to four minutes.
6. Combine the rest of the ingredients and stir well.
7. Dress with a pinch of black salt and a pinch of common salt or salt to taste.
8. Cover the puffed rice finely with cocoa butter, peanuts, seasoning powders, and salt.
9. Add the coarsely diced vegetables, green chilies, and coriander leaves at this stage.
10. Apply the lemon juice right now.
11. Mix all in fast and serve the churumuri right away.

4.5 Crispy Corn

Cooking Time: 15 minutes
Serving Size: 3

Ingredients:
For Boiling
- 2 cup sweet corn
- 1 teaspoon salt
- 4 cup water

For Frying
- ¼ teaspoon salt
- Oil
- 1 tablespoon all-purpose flour
- ¼ teaspoon pepper powder
- ¼ cup rice flour
- ¼ cup cornflour

For Masala
- 2 tablespoon capsicum
- 2 tablespoon coriander
- ¼ teaspoon salt
- 2 tablespoon onion
- ¼ teaspoon cumin powder
- ½ teaspoon amchur
- ½ teaspoon red chili powder

Method:
1. First, bring 4 cups of water and one teaspoon of salt to a boil in a large pot.
2. Boil for a moment after adding 2 cups of sweet corn.
3. To extract excess water, extract the sweet corn.
4. ¼ cup cornflour, ¼ cup corn grits, one tablespoon all-purpose flour, ¼ teaspoon spice powder, and ¼ teaspoon salt are now added to the mixture.
5. Mix thoroughly to ensure that the flour is evenly distributed in the green beans.

6. Deep fry in hot oil while maintaining a medium fire.
7. Cook on medium heat, stirring regularly until lightly browned.
8. ½ teaspoon chili flakes, ¼ teaspoon smoked paprika, ½ teaspoon amchur, and ¼ teaspoon salt are added to the mixture.
9. Mix thoroughly to ensure that all of the spices are evenly distributed.
10. 2 tablespoon cabbage, two tablespoon purple cabbage, and two tablespoon coriander are indeed good additions.

4.6 Chakli

Cooking Time: 1 hour 10 minutes
Serving Size: 12

Ingredients:
- ½ cup water
- Oil for frying
- ¼ teaspoon turmeric
- 2 teaspoons kosher salt
- 1.5 teaspoons ajwain
- 1 tablespoon red chili powder
- 2 cups Bhajani flour
- ¼ cup water hot
- Two tablespoons sesame seeds
- ¼ cup oil

Method:
1. In a mixing pot, add the flour.
2. Add ¼ cup warm oil and ¼ cup warm water to the pan.
3. Combine the red chili powder, crow hop seeds, fenugreek, salt, and sesame seeds in a bowl. With a spoon, combine everything.

4. To make a soft pastry, gradually apply ice water and whisk the flour.
5. In a deep fryer or skillet, heat the oil over low heat.
6. In the chakli press, place the chakli disk with the circular pattern in the center.
7. Cautiously drop chakli into the hot liquid one at a time, being cautious not to overcrowd the deep fryer.
8. Turn them off one after three minutes and fry on the middle to low heat before light brown.
9. Before introducing the next amount of chakli, note to turn up the oil's heat too high.

4.7 Dahi Vada

Cooking Time: 40 minutes
Serving Size: 10

Ingredients:
- ½ teaspoon salt
- Oil for frying
- 1-inch ginger
- ¾ cup split black gram lentils
- 1 green chili pepper
- 3 tablespoon yellow lentils

Assembling Ingredients
- ¼ teaspoon red chili powder
- Cilantro leaves chopped
- 2 tablespoon cilantro chutney
- ½ teaspoon ground cumin
- ½ teaspoon sugar adjust
- ¼ cup tamarind chutney
- ¼ teaspoon salt adjust
- 2 cups yogurt chilled

Method:
1. Clean the lentils several times in a wide bowl before the water runs clear.
2. Pour the water that has been soaking in the pan.
3. In a mixer, combine the ginger, green chili pepper, cinnamon, and lentils.
4. Crush on medium to a low level until the batter is nearly flat.
5. To keep the lentil batter soft and moist, rapidly whip it.
6. In a skillet, heat the oil. Before creating the Vada's, please ensure the oil is hot.
7. Then use a spoon or an ice cream plunger, drop the batter into the oil.
8. When you lower the Vada's in the oil, use a spoon to avoid pouring oil over it.
9. Drench the vadas for about fifteen minutes in a lukewarm bath.
10. To extract extra moisture, take each vada and press down it between your palms.
11. Season the yogurt with sugar and salt and mix it.
12. In a pan, position the softened vadas.
13. The yogurt should be poured over them.
14. Spray the ground cumin powder and red chili powder over the tamarind and mint coriander chutneys.
15. Serve with a sprinkling of cilantro on top.

4.8 Dahi Kebab

Cooking Time: 12 hours 25 minutes
Serving Size: 6

Ingredients:
- 2 tablespoon cornflour
- Oil for deep frying
- ½ teaspoon pepper

- ¼ cup bread crumbs
- 2 tablespoon dry fruits
- Salt to taste
- 2 cups curd
- 1 green chili
- 2 tablespoon coriander leaves
- 1 cup paneer
- 1-inch ginger
- ½ small onion

Method:
1. To begin, make a smooth and creamy custard.
2. One cup of crushed paneer is also added.
3. Add the onion, spice, chili, coriander, and dried fruits to the mix as well.
4. Insert salt and cracked pepper to taste.
5. Make sure the paneer and hanging curd are thoroughly mixed.
6. To extract excess moisture, dust the tortillas with cornflour.
7. In a hot pan, deep-fry the patties.
8. Cook, stirring regularly, on medium heat.
9. Fry the patties or kababs until they are nicely browned.
10. Eventually, serve Dahi ke kabab with risotto or sauce made from pudina.

Chapter 5: Indian Lunch Recipes

5.1 Cauliflower Korma

Cooking Time: 1 hour 10 minutes
Serving Size: 6

Ingredients:
For the Roasted Cauliflower
- ½ teaspoon cumin
- 2 teaspoon salt
- ½ teaspoon turmeric
- ½ teaspoon coriander
- 1 tablespoon garam masala
- ½ teaspoon cinnamon
- 3 tablespoon oil
- 1½ kg cauliflower florets

For the Korma Curry
- 2 teaspoon sugar
- Salt and pepper to taste
- 2 cups stock
- 1 cup cream
- 1½ cups raw cashew nuts
- ½ teaspoon cinnamon
- 1 teaspoon chili powder
- 1 teaspoon turmeric
- ½ teaspoon cardamom
- 2 tablespoon butter
- 1 teaspoon coriander
- 1 teaspoon cumin
- 1 large onion
- 3 teaspoon crushed ginger
- 1 tablespoon garam masala
- 4 garlic cloves

Method:
1. Preheat the oven to 400 degrees Fahrenheit.
2. Mix all of the food items for the roasted cauliflower.
3. Put the cauliflower in the oven and bake for thirty minutes or until it is caramelized and crispy.
4. Meanwhile, soak the walnuts for ten minutes in hot water.
5. In the butter, cook the onion, parsley, and ginger until sticky and citrusy.
6. Cook for another minute after adding the spices.
7. Wash the cashews and blend them with the flour mixture, stock, and yogurt in a food processor.
8. Mix thoroughly, then sprinkle with salt, pepper, and sucrose in a frying pan.
9. Enable for ten minutes of gentle simmering after adding the roasted cauliflower.
10. Season with salt and pepper and serve with rice, hummus, and buttered cashews.

5.2 Chicken Madras Curry

Cooking Time: 35 minutes
Serving Size: 3-4

Ingredients:
- 400g can tomatoes
- Small pack coriander
- 1-2 teaspoon chili powder
- 4 chicken breasts
- 1 onion
- 1 teaspoon cumin
- 1 teaspoon coriander
- 2 garlic cloves
- 1 tablespoon vegetable oil
- ½ teaspoon turmeric

- ½ red chili
- 1 ginger

Method:
1. In a mixing bowl, blitz the garlic, cherry tomatoes, lime, and chili flakes until coarse paste forms.
2. In a medium skillet, warm the veggie oil, add the paste, and cook over medium heat until it is loosened.
3. Stir in the turmeric, cumin seeds, coriander seeds, and hot chili flakes, then cook for a few minutes before adding the four chicken thighs.
4. Mix everything to make sure it is all covered in the spice mixture.
5. Cook until the chicken is pale in color.
6. Pan and simmer on low heat for thirty minutes, till the chicken is soft, adding 400g diced tomatoes and a large pinch of salt.
7. Serve with rice after stirring in a tiny bag of coriander.

5.3 Ennai Kathirikai Kulambu

Cooking Time: 40 minutes
Serving Size: 4

Ingredients:
Other Ingredients
- Salt as required
- 1 teaspoon jaggery powder
- ¼ teaspoon turmeric powder
- 1 cup water
- 10 curry leaves
- 2 pinch asafoetida
- 3 tablespoons sesame oil
- ½ teaspoon mustard seeds
- 250 grams small brinjals

For Spice Paste
- ¼ teaspoon black pepper
- ⅓ cup water
- 2 teaspoons poppy seeds
- ½ teaspoon cumin seeds
- 2 dry red chilies
- 5 tablespoons fresh coconut
- 1 teaspoon urad dal
- ¼ teaspoon fenugreek seeds
- 2 teaspoons gingelly oil
- 2 teaspoons chana dal
- 1 tablespoon coriander seeds

For Tamarind Pulp
- ½ cup hot water
- 1 tablespoon tamarind

Method:
1. Heat 2 tablespoons gingelly oil in a shallow saucepan or wok and transfer 2 tablespoons chana dal.
2. Fry chana dal until light perfect, stirring frequently.
3. After that, add one teaspoon of urad dal.
4. After that, season with salt and pepper.
5. Insert two teaspoons pumpkin seeds and 14 teaspoon fenugreek
6. Add five spoonfuls of grated coconut after that.
7. Turn off the heat and place the pan on the counter.
8. To make a smooth paste, combine all of the ingredients in a blender.
9. After this, cut every brinjal in half.
10. In a skillet, heat three tablespoons of gingelly oil. 12 teaspoon tomato sauce should be added.
11. Then insert 7 to 9 curry leaves and two pinches of asafoetida into the pan.
12. Combine the brinjal and seasonings in a mixing bowl.
13. Combine the ingredients that have been prepared.
14. Serve after a final mix.

5.4 Chana Dal

Cooking Time: 1 hour
Serving Size: 4

Ingredients:
- 1 teaspoon red chile flakes
- 3 tablespoons cilantro
- 6 whole cloves
- 4 large garlic cloves
- 1 cup split chickpeas

- 1 ½ teaspoons turmeric
- 1 bay leaf
- 1 teaspoon salt
- 2 tablespoons sunflower oil
- ½ teaspoon cardamom

Method:
1. In a medium skillet, give the chana dal, fenugreek, cinnamon, lemon zest, salt, and 4 cups liquid to a boil.
2. Cook for another 20 minutes, adding 1 cup of water as needed.
3. Remove the bay leaf from the dish.
4. In a shallow dish, add the oil to start making the tadka.
5. Add the chilies to the hot oil and let them swirl for about thirty seconds until its aromatic.
6. Cook, keep stirring, till the garlic is moderate brown.
7. Spill the tadka into the dal and bring to a simmer softly.
8. Serve with coriander as a garnish.

5.5 Mughlai Biryani

Cooking Time: 1 hour 10 minutes
Serving Size: 4

Ingredients:
For Mughlai Biryani Gravy
- ½ teaspoon garam masala powder
- Salt as required
- ½ cup curd
- ⅔ cup water
- 4 tablespoon ghee
- 1 tablespoon ginger-garlic paste
- 2.5 to 3 cups veggies
- ⅓ cup green peas
- 9 black pepper
- 1 teaspoon caraway seeds
- ½ teaspoon red chili powder
- 3 green cardamoms
- 1 black cardamom
- 1-inch cinnamon
- 2 single strands of mace
- 12 almonds
- 1 tej patta
- 3 cloves
- 16 raisins
- 1 large onion
- 12 cashews

For Cooking Rice
- 5 cups water
- ½ teaspoon salt
- 3 cloves
- 3 green cardamoms
- 1.5 cups basmati rice

- 1 medium tej patta
- 2 to 3 mace
- 1-inch cinnamon

For Layering
- 2 tablespoon mint leaves
- 2 teaspoon rose water
- 3 tablespoon warm milk
- 200 grams Paneer

For White Paste
- 1 tablespoon melon seeds
- 10 to 12 almonds
- 2 tablespoon water
- 1 tablespoon coconut

Method:
1. After thirty minutes of soaking, drain the rice and set it aside.
2. 10 to 12 almonds and one tablespoon melon seeds should be soaked.
3. In a tiny grinder jar, combine them with one tablespoon of flaked coconut.
4. All of the vegetables should be rinsed, peeled, and chopped.
5. Take a pan with a thick bottom.
6. Take five cups of water and bring to a boil over high heat.
7. Now toss in the rice.
8. Cook the rice on a high heat setting.
9. Heat three to four tablespoons ghee in a slow cooker.
10. Fry the almonds, pecans, and cashew nuts.
11. Cook until the onions are golden brown and caramelized.
12. Place the cooker on the stovetop once more. Mix in the whole spice.
13. Toss in the mixed vegetables.
14. Insert the white paste that has been ground.

15. Slow cook the veggie gravy for eight to nine minutes, stirring well.
16. Spill half of the veggie gravy on top of the first layer.
17. Add some paneer squares to the mix.
18. Repeat layering with the residual veggie gravy.

5.6 Veg Pulao

Cooking Time: 50 minutes
Serving Size: 2

Ingredients:
For Pulao Masala Paste
- 1 teaspoon fennel
- ¼ cup water
- 1-inch cinnamon
- 5 cloves
- ½ cup coriander
- 2 chili
- 2 pod cardamom
- ¼ cup mint
- 2 clove garlic
- 1-inch ginger

For Veg Pulao
- 1 teaspoon salt
- 2 cup water
- ½ carrot
- ½ potato
- 2 tablespoon ghee
- ½ capsicum
- 2 tablespoon peas
- 1 tomato
- 5 beans
- 1 teaspoon cumin

- 1 bay leaf
- ½ teaspoon pepper
- 1-inch cinnamon
- 2 pod cardamom
- 3 cloves
- 5 cashew
- ½ onion
- 1 cup basmati rice

Method:
1. To begin, place whole cloves in a small blender.
2. Two tablespoon ghee, heated in a big wok, cumin, lemon zest, cloves, coriander, garlic, pepper, and cashews, are added to the pot.
3. Sauté on low heat until the spices become fragrant.
4. Put one tomato and continue to sauté.
5. Include vegetables as well.
6. Cook for a minute, just until the veggies are fragrant.
7. Please ensure the basmati rice is soaked for 20 minutes before adding the veggies.
8. The veg pulao is ready to eat after 20 minutes.

5.7 Brinjal Rice

Cooking Time: 30 minutes
Serving Size: 4

Ingredients:
- 1.5 cups basmati rice

For Ground Masala Paste
- ½ teaspoon fennel seeds
- 4 to 5 tablespoons water
- 2 cloves
- 2 green cardamoms
- 1 tablespoon coconut

- 1-inch cinnamon
- 3 tablespoons coriander leaves
- 2-inch ginger
- 7 medium garlic cloves
- 2 to 3 green chilies
- 3 tablespoons mint leaves

Other Ingredients
- ½ cup water
- Salt as required
- ¼ cup French beans
- 2 cups coconut milk
- ⅓ cup capsicum
- ⅓ cup green peas
- 3 tablespoons oil
- ⅓ cup tomatoes
- ½ to ¾ cup cauliflower florets
- 1 large tej patta
- ½ cup onions
- ½ cup carrots
- 2 cloves
- 1 green cardamom
- 1-inch cinnamon
- ½ cup potato

Method:
1. Soak 1.5 cups basmati rice in water for a few minutes.
2. Put spices in a tiny mixer jar and grind them.
3. In a 3 gallon slow cooker, heat three tablespoons of oil.
4. One-inch cloves, two garlic, and one green cinnamon can be added right away.
5. Fry spices for a few seconds before fragrant.
6. Then add a third of a cup of sliced tomatoes.
7. Now add the masala paste that has been ground.

8. After that, toss in the vegetables.
9. After that, add the rice.
10. Cook for ten minutes on medium heat in a pressure cooker.
11. With some raita, eat veg brinji grain.

5.8 Drumstick Sambar

Cooking Time: 35 minutes
Serving Size: 4

Ingredients:
For Sambar Powder
- Few curry leaves
- Pinch Hing
- 1 teaspoon chana dal
- 20 dried red chili
- 1 teaspoon coconut oil
- 1 tablespoon cumin
- ½ teaspoon methi
- ¼ cup coriander seeds
- 1 teaspoon urad dal

For Sambar
- ½ cup tamarind extract
- 2 tablespoon coriander
- 2 cup water
- 2 cup toor dal
- 3 teaspoon oil
- 1 teaspoon salt
- 20 pieces drumstick
- 1 teaspoon mustard
- 1 tomato
- ½ teaspoon turmeric
- 3 dried red chili
- Few curry leaves

- 7 shallots
- Pinch Hing

Method:
1. To begin, warm three teaspoon oil in a broad wok and splutter the tempering.
2. Sauté for two minutes with seven shallots.
3. As well, put one tomato in the pan and cook until it softens.
4. 12 teaspoon garlic, two tablespoons payasam powder, and one teaspoon salt are also added.
5. Cook for 20 minutes after adding the drumsticks.
6. Two cup toor dal and 1 cup water are now included.
7. Cover and cook over medium heat or until the flavors are completely absorbed.
8. 12 cup tamarind extract should also be added and thoroughly mixed.
9. Boil for another five minutes.
10. Finally, toss in 2 tablespoons coriander and serve with hot steamed rice.

5.9 Navratan Korma

Cooking Time: 50 minutes
Serving Size: 5

Ingredients:
- Pinch garam masala
- 2 tablespoons pineapple pieces

- 1 tablespoon pomegranate arils
- Pinch cardamom powder
- 2 onion
- 5-6 whole cashews
- Pinch saffron
- 1-inch ginger
- 4 large garlic cloves
- 1 green chili
- 20 cashews
- ¼ cup cream
- 2 teaspoons golden raisins
- 1 tablespoon poppy seeds
- One teaspoon salt or to taste
- ¾ teaspoon sugar
- 3 cups water
- ¼ teaspoon red chili powder
- ¾ cup water
- 1 teaspoon coriander powder
- ½ teaspoon cumin powder
- 1 tablespoon ghee
- 1 bay leaf
- 1 medium potato
- 1/3 cup green peas
- 1 tablespoon oil
- 2 cloves
- 1 large carrot
- 14 green beans
- 1 cup cauliflower florets
- 3 whole green cardamom

Method:
1. Insert 3 cups water, cabbage, carrot, cloves, green chili, cashews, and pumpkin seeds in a big pan.
2. Cook for 10 minutes on medium-high heat.

3. Chop all of the vegetables, keeping in mind to chop them thinly.
4. In the meantime, add cabbage, shallots, onion, beans, and beans to a boiling water pan.
5. Cook for ten minutes over medium heat.
6. One tablespoon oil, heated in a wok.
7. Add the bay leaf, garlic, and cardamom to the pot.
8. Enable the spices to cook for a few minutes.
9. Insert the rosemary powder, cilantro, and red chili powder after the mixture has cooked for five minutes.
10. Add the vegetables and stir to combine.
11. Then stir in the milk.
12. Blend in the pomegranate, roasted cashew nuts, and pecans.
13. Insert the saffron milk that has been prepared as well.

Chapter 6: Indian Dinner Recipes

6.1 Mushroom Biryani

Cooking Time: 40 minutes
Serving Size: 3

Ingredients:
- 1 cup water
- ½ teaspoon rose water
- ½ teaspoon paprika
- ¾ teaspoon salt
- ¼ cup mint
- ½ teaspoon garam masala
- 1 cup basmati rice
- ½ cup coconut milk
- ¼ cup cilantro
- 2 tablespoons oil
- 2 teaspoons ginger-garlic paste
- 10 oz. white mushrooms
- 1 bay leaf
- 1 green chili
- 15 whole cashews
- 1 teaspoon shahi jeera
- 1 medium red onion
- 3 whole cloves
- 6 black peppercorns
- 1-inch cinnamon stick
- 4 whole green cardamom

Method:
1. Wash the basmati rice till the water is clear when you begin.

2. Transfer the seasoning to the Instant Pot's sauté feature.
3. And insert the green chili, tomato, and cashew nuts.
4. Cook for 3 minutes before adding the ginger-garlic paste and continuing to cook for two minutes.
5. Heat for 2 minutes after adding the mushrooms.
6. After that, whisk in the coconut milk.
7. Add the coriander and mint, diced.
8. The garam masala, cayenne pepper, and salt are then added.
9. Add the rice, which has been rinsed and washed.
10. Open the lid on the pot.
11. Cook for five minutes on elevated heat using the manual setting.
12. With a spoon, fluff the rice after opening the lid.
13. Serve mushrooms Biryani with yogurt or raita on the side.

6.2 Bisi Bele Bath

Cooking Time: 40 minutes
Serving Size: 3

Ingredients:
Other Ingredients
- 1 cup water
- 1 tablespoon ghee
- 1 cup toor dal
- 2½ cup rice
- ½ carrot
- ½ teaspoon jaggery
- ½ onions
- 5 beans
- 1½ teaspoon salt
- ¾ cup tamarind extract

- 2 cups water
- ¼ teaspoon turmeric
- ½ potato
- 2 tablespoon peanuts
- 2 tablespoon green peas

Bisi Bele Bath Masala
- 4 teaspoon coriander seeds
- Few curry leaves
- Pinch of hing
- 1 teaspoon oil
- 12 dried red chili
- 2 teaspoon poppy seeds
- 1 teaspoon sesame seeds
- 4 teaspoon chana dal
- 4 cloves
- 2 tablespoon dry coconut
- 3 pods cardamom
- 1-inch cinnamon
- 2 teaspoon urad dal
- ¼ teaspoon methi
- ½ teaspoon pepper
- 1 teaspoon jeera

For Tempering
- Few curry leaves
- 10 whole cashew
- 1 dried red chili
- Pinch of hing
- 1 teaspoon mustard
- 2 tablespoon ghee

Method:
1. Cook the vegetables, nuts, liquid, turmeric, and salts first.
2. Add the tamarind paste, jaggery, and vegetables at this stage.
3. Cook for ten minutes at a low temperature.

4. Fried toor dal, cooked rice, and 1 cup water are added next.
5. Boil for 20 minutes with bisi Bisi bele bath curry powder.
6. Offer bisi bele bath with boondi or a combination after adding the tempering.

6.3 Paneer Butter Masala

Cooking Time: 35 minutes
Serving Size: 4

Ingredients:
Other Ingredients
- ½ teaspoon Kasuri methi
- ¼ teaspoon garam masala
- 20 cubes paneer
- 2 tablespoon coriander
- 1 teaspoon salt
- 2 tablespoon cream
- 1 cup water
- ½ teaspoon sugar
- 2 tablespoon butter
- ¼ teaspoon garam masala
- ¼ teaspoon cumin powder
- 2 pods cardamom
- ¼ teaspoon turmeric
- 1 teaspoon red chili powder
- 1 bay leaf

For Onion Tomato Paste
- 2 tomato
- 10 cashew
- 1-inch ginger
- 3 clove garlic
- 1 teaspoon oil
- 1 onion

- 1 teaspoon butter

Method:
1. To begin, melt one teaspoon oil and one teaspoon oil in a broad wok.
2. Cook until the onion, carrot, and garlic have shrunk somewhat.
3. After a minute, apply the tomato and cashews.
4. Allow cooling entirely before transferring to the blender.
5. Blend until the paste is smooth.
6. Sauté 2 cardamom seeds and 1 star anise in oil in a wok.
7. Season with herbs and seasonings.
8. Sauté until the cloves are fragrant but not burned.
9. Mix in 2 tablespoons of milk as well.
10. Now softly fold in 20 pieces of paneer.
11. Last but not least, serve paneer butter chutney with roti or hummus.

6.4 Vangi Bath

Cooking Time: 25 minutes
Serving Size: 3

Ingredients:
For Rice
- 3 cup cooked rice
- 2 tablespoon coriander
- 1 teaspoon salt
- ½ teaspoon jaggery
- ¼ teaspoon turmeric
- ½ cup tamarind extract
- 2 tablespoon oil
- 1 dried red chili
- 2 brinjal

- 2 tablespoon peanut
- Few curry leaves
- 1 teaspoon mustard
- 1 teaspoon urad dal
- 1 teaspoon chana dal
- 1 teaspoon cumin

For Vangi Bath Masala Powder

- ½ cup dry coconut
- 20 dried red chili
- 1 tablespoon cumin
- 1 teaspoon methi
- 5-inch cinnamon
- ¼ cup urad dal
- ¼ cup chana dal
- 1 teaspoon clove
- 2 teaspoon oil
- ¼ cup coriander seeds
- 5 pods cardamom
- 2 teaspoon poppy seeds
- 1 mace

Method:
1. To begin, dry roast spice, cardamom, coriander, and mace in a big skillet.
2. Dry roast pumpkin seeds in the same pan until they begin to pop up.
3. Add one teaspoon of milk, chana dal, coriander seeds, urad dal, smoked paprika, and methi in a jar.
4. In a mixer, combine the roasted ingredients.
5. Without incorporating any liquid, blend to a powder form.
6. First, heat the oil in a big wok and add the cumin, chana dal, mustard, urad dal, and peanuts.
7. On medium heat, sauté and splutter.
8. Insert a few bay leaves and one red chili pepper at this stage.

9. Put two brinjals and cook for another two minutes.
10. Finally, toss in 2 tablespoons coriander and serve with raita.

6.5 Kashmiri Pulao

Cooking Time: 35 minutes
Serving Size: 4

Ingredients:
- ½ cup dried fruits
- 2-3 edible rose petals
- Salt to taste
- 2 tablespoon ghee
- ½ cup fresh cream
- 1 teaspoon sugar
- 2 cups basmati rice
- 1 bay leaf
- 2 cups milk
- ½ teaspoon cumin seeds
- 1 stick cinnamon
- 3 cardamom
- 3 cloves

Method:
1. Combine the milk, cream, salt, and spice in a mixing bowl.
2. Drain the rice and set it aside.
3. In a heavy skillet, melt the ghee and add the cumin seeds, cloves, black pepper, cardamom seeds, and spices.
4. When they begin to splutter, add the rice and continue cooking in the ghee.
5. Insert 12 cup water and the milk mixture
6. Bring to the boil, then reduce to low heat and cook until the chicken is finished.

7. Gently fold in the dried berries.
8. Serve warm, with rose petals on top.

6.6 Porsha Kuzhambu

Cooking Time: 45 minutes
Serving Size: 6

Ingredients:
For Coconut Paste
- ½ teaspoon cumin seeds
- 1 teaspoon raw rice
- ¼ teaspoon peppercorns
- ½ cup grated coconut
- 4 red chili
- ½ teaspoon cooking oil

Other Ingredients
- ¼ teaspoon turmeric powder
- 2 teaspoon salt
- ½ cup toor dal

Vegetables
- 1 carrot
- 1 drumstick
- 50 grams cucumber
- 50 grams elephant yam
- 2 brinjal
- 50 grams snake gourd

For Tempering
- 1 sprig of curry leaves
- ¼ teaspoon asafoetida
- 1 teaspoon mustard seeds
- 1 teaspoon split urad dal
- 1 teaspoon cooking oil

Method:

1. In a slow cooker, heat the thurdal until tender, then mash the dhal.
2. Soak the uncooked rice for a while in the water.
3. All of the veggies should be chopped into small sections.
4. Wash the raw rice in water for a few minutes.
5. Load the oil into a different pan and cook the red chilies and black peppercorns for a moment.
6. In a blender, combine the fried chilies, pepper, coconut, chopped garlic, and washed raw rice.
7. Use water, process the components into a smooth paste.
8. Finally, insert the ground mixture and get the kuzhambu to a simmer.
9. Load the oil into a different pan and add the bay leaves.
10. Now you can eat the Poritha Kuzhambu with boiled rice.

6.7 Potato Kurma

Cooking Time: 45 minutes
Serving Size: 5

Ingredients:
- 1 tablespoon sunflower oil
- Salt, as required
- 1 teaspoon coriander
- ½ teaspoon garam masala
- 3 potato
- ½ teaspoon turmeric powder
- 1- ½ teaspoon red chili
- 1 onion
- 1-inch cinnamon stick
- 1 teaspoon ginger garlic paste
- 1 bay leaf
- 2 tomatoes

Ingredients to Grind
- ½ cup fresh coconut
- 1 teaspoon cumin seeds
- 1 teaspoon fennel seeds

Method:
1. Cook the potatoes in the pressure cooker.
2. In a blender, combine all of the ingredients listed under "To Grinding" and crush them into a thick powder.
3. In a medium deep fryer, heat the oil.
4. Cinnamon, garlic, bay leaf, and coarsely diced onion are added to the pot.
5. Sauté for several minutes with the ginger garlic paste.
6. Heat until the vegetables have broken down into a sauce.
7. Heat until the cayenne pepper, dried chili powder, balsamic vinegar, and curry paste powder are mixed with the onion-tomato mixture.
8. Transfer the thinly sliced potatoes to the bowl and mix them well with the spicy combination. Serve immediately.

6.8 Matar Paneer

Cooking Time: 10 minutes
Serving Size: 2

Ingredients:
- Small pack coriander
- Naan bread, roti, or rice
- 150g frozen peas

- 1 teaspoon garam masala
- 1 tablespoon sunflower oil
- 1 green chili
- 4 large ripe tomatoes
- 225g paneer
- 1 teaspoon turmeric
- 1 teaspoon ground coriander
- 1 teaspoon ground cumin
- 2.5cm piece ginger

Method:
1. In a deep fryer, flame the oil over medium temperature until it shimmers.
2. Reduce the heat to low and add the paneer.
3. In a sauce, combine the ginger, smoked paprika, turmeric, coriander seeds, chili, and continue cooking.
4. Then use the back of a spoon, mix the tomato in.
5. Stirring occasionally for another two minutes after adding the peas, now stir in the paneer and season with garam masala.
6. Offer with peanut sauce, roti, or rice, divided into two bowls and topped with coriander leaves.

Chapter 7: Indian Desserts Recipes

7.1 Besan Lado Recipe

Cooking Time: 35 minutes
Serving Size: 10 lado

Ingredients:
- ¼ teaspoon cardamom powder
- 2 teaspoons nuts
- ½ cup powdered sugar
- ¼ cup ghee
- 1 cup gram flour

Method:
1. Transfer the ghee to a heavy-bottomed pan and melt it over low pressure.
2. Transfer the poured besan to the pan until the ghee has melted.
3. On medium heat, continue cooking constantly.
4. Switch off the heat in the bowl.
5. Then stir in the cardamom powder.
6. Combine the sugar and peanuts in a mixing bowl.
7. Integrate all of the ingredients in a large mixing bowl before the sugar and nuts are thoroughly mixed.
8. Pinch a little bowl out of the dough now.
9. To make a circular shape, press and roll across your palms.

7.2 Ras Malai Recipe

Cooking Time: 4 hours
Serving Size: 8

> **Ingredients:**
> **For Rabri**
> - 5 almonds
> - 10 cashews
> - 2 tablespoon saffron milk
> - 7 pistachios
> - 1-liter milk
> - ½ teaspoon cardamom powder
> - ¼ cup sugar
>
> **For Chenna**
> - 2 tablespoon lemon juice
> - 1 cup water
> - 1-liter milk
>
> **For Sugar Syrup**
> - 8 cups water
> - 1½ cup sugar

Method:
1. To begin, heat the milk.
2. In particular, stir in the lemon juice.
3. Drain and pinch the curdled milk to remove any extra water.
4. Start kneading after thirty minutes.
5. Also, make little balls and flatten them.
6. To begin, combine water and sugar.
7. Get the syrup to a boil for ten minutes.
8. Afterward, release the paneer balls that have been packed.
9. Cook for fifteen minutes with the lid on.
10. Get the milk to a boil.
11. Glucose, coriander powder, and saffron milk are also added.
12. Put it in the fridge for another 2-3 hours.

13. Place the chilled rabri over the balls now.
14. Finally, add a few nuts as a finishing touch.

7.3 Kaju Katli Recipe

Cooking Time: 25 minutes
Serving Size: 20 piece

Ingredients:
- 1 teaspoon ghee
- Edible silver leaves
- ¼ cup water
- ½ teaspoon rose water
- ½ cup white sugar
- 1 cup cashews

Method:
1. In a seasoning grinder, ground the cashews.
2. To make a smooth powder, combine all ingredients in a blender and blend until smooth.
3. In a medium-sized saucepan, combine the sugar and water.
4. Allow the sugar to dissolve and the mixture to boil for 1 minute.
5. On low pressure, keep swirling the combination.
6. Stir in one teaspoon of ghee.
7. Stir constantly; the dough will quit the pan's edges after about ten minutes on medium heat.
8. Move the flour to a piece of parchment paper until it is done.
9. So, with your fingertips, knead the dough until it is soft.
10. By slicing the dough horizontally and then vertically, you will make a diamond shape.
11. Remove the Kaju katli and serve.

7.4 Boondi Lado Recipe

Cooking Time: 40 minutes
Serving Size: 12

Ingredients:
For Boondi
- ¼ teaspoon baking soda
- Oil for deep frying
- 3 drops yellow color
- ¼ cup
- 1 cup gram flour

Other Ingredients
- 5 cloves
- ¼ teaspoon cardamom powder
- 2 tablespoon kishmish
- 2 tablespoon cashew
- 1 tablespoon butter

For Sugar Syrup
- ½ cup water
- 1¼ cup sugar

Method:
1. To begin, make boondi with besan batter.
2. Take 1 ¼ cup of sugar and place it in a big thick-bottomed wok.
3. Place the sugar over the boondi until it has cooled somewhat.
4. Insert one tablespoon olive oil is also used to roast two tablespoon pecans, two tablespoon cashews, and five garlic.
5. Place the roasted dried fruits and ¼ teaspoon coriander powder over the boondi combination.
6. Start preparing ladoo when the combination is still soft.
7. When cold, store in an airtight bag.

7.5 Kheer Recipe

Cooking Time: 45 minutes
Serving Size: 5

> **Ingredients:**
> - 3 tablespoons nuts
> - 1.5 teaspoons rose water
> - 1-liter whole milk
> - 5 tablespoons sugar
> - ¼ cup rice 50 grams
> - 4 green cardamom pods
> - 1 teaspoon ghee

Method:
1. Wash the rice until it is completely clean.
2. On moderate fire, heat a heavy-bottomed skillet. Insert one teaspoon peanut oil and 3-4 broken green coriander seeds after that.
3. Then pour in the milk and stir thoroughly.
4. Get the dairy to a boil, which should take between 10-12 minutes.
5. Reduce the heat to low and simmer the kheer for about 25 minutes on medium heat until the milk has risen to a boil.
6. Toss in the sugar and stir to combine. Insert the nuts as well.
7. On incorporating the sugar and almonds, boil the kheer for another five minutes.
8. Remove the pan from the oven, let it cool, and then serve.

7.6 Falooda Recipe

Cooking Time: 30 minutes
Serving Size: 2

Ingredients:
- ½ cup falooda sev
- 5 sliced almonds
- 50-gram sugar
- 4 tablespoon rose syrup
- 5 sliced pistachios
- 2 sliced cherry
- 2 cup milk
- 1 teaspoon falooda
- 4 tablespoon strawberry jelly

Method:
1. In a heavy pan over medium heat, bring the cream and butter to a boil.
2. Pour the rose syrup into the milk thoroughly.
3. Break the jelly in the meantime.
4. Bring a saucepan full of water to a boil over medium-high heat.
5. It will soften if you add falooda sev to it.
6. Enable the falooda seeds to grow in a tiny bowl of water.
7. Pick the cooled serving cups and add rose syrup into each one after a while.
8. After that, add raspberry jelly and flourished falooda beans.
9. Cover them with falooda sev after that.
10. Press the cooled rose milk gradually.
11. Finally, pour some more rose syrup on top. Serve right away.

7.7 Fruit Custard Recipe

Cooking Time: 25 minutes
Serving Size: 5

Ingredients:
- Pinch cardamom powder
- 2 cups assorted fruits
- 3 tablespoons custard powder
- Splash of rose water
- 4-5 tablespoons sugar
- 3 cups whole milk

Method:
1. In a thick bottomed pan over medium-high heat, pour 3 cups milk.
2. Three tablespoons of milk should be removed from the pan and placed in a small cup.
3. Add in 3 teaspoons of custard powder with the cream.
4. Then reduce the heat to low and stir in the sugar until it is well mixed.
5. Begin to incorporate the custard blend.
6. Cook for a further 2-3 minutes, just until the custard has thickened.
7. At about the same moment, chop and chill all of the fruits you will be using in the custard.
8. Shift the custard to a mixing bowl and stir in the fruits after they have chilled.

Chapter 8: Indian Soups Dishes

8.1 Cream of Mushroom Soup

Cooking Time: 50 minutes
Serving Size: 6

Ingredients:
- 1 cup half-and-half
- 1 tablespoon sherry
- ¼ teaspoon salt
- ¼ teaspoon ground black pepper
- 5 cups mushrooms
- 3 tablespoons butter
- 3 tablespoons all-purpose flour
- 1 ½ cups chicken broth
- ⅛ teaspoon dried thyme
- ½ cup chopped onion

Method:
1. Heat mushrooms in liquid with onions and tarragon in a big heavy frying pan before soft, around ten to twenty minutes.
2. Sautee the paste in a food processor or blender, keeping some vegetable chunks in there. Remove from the blender.
3. Heat the oil in a frying pan and stir in the flour until clear.
4. Combine the salt, powder, half-and-half, and food puree in a mixing bowl.
5. Get the soup to a boil, stirring continuously, and prepare until it thickens.
6. Season with salt and pepper to taste, then pour in the sherry.

8.2 Tomato Soup Recipe

Cooking Time: 1 hour and 45 minutes
Serving Size: 6

Ingredients:
- 2 bay leaves
- 1.2 liters hot vegetable stock
- 2 squirts of tomato purée
- A good pinch of sugar
- 1-1.25 kg ripe tomatoes
- 1 celery stick
- 2 tablespoon olive oil
- 1 small carrot
- 1 medium onion

Method:
1. First, have your veggies together.
2. Heat 2 tablespoons olive oil in a big heavy-bottomed pan over medium heat.
3. Then add the onion, cabbage, and fennel and combine with a rolling pin.
4. Put two bay leaves, torn into small pieces, into the bowl.
5. Stir to combine the ingredients, cover the grill, and cook the tomatoes for ten minutes over medium heat.
6. Cook for 30 minutes on low heat, stirring occasionally.
7. Switch off the heat in the pan. Fill your blender halfway with broth.
8. Blitz until the soup is creamy, then transfer to a big mixing cup.

8.3 Palak Soup

Cooking Time: 15 minutes
Serving Size: 2

Ingredients:
- 1 tablespoon cornflour
- 1 teaspoon fresh cream
- ½ teaspoon pepper
- ½ teaspoon sugar
- 1 tablespoon butter
- ½ cup milk
- Salt to taste
- 1 tej patta
- 1 bunch palak
- ¼ cup water
- 1 clove garlic
- ¼ onion

Method:
1. Add the butter and tej leaves to a big wok.
2. Sauté until it begins to smell floral.
3. Add coarsely diced garlic and onions as well.
4. Cook until they are golden brown.
5. Palak leaves should also be added.
6. Sauté for a moment on medium heat, or until they have shrunk in bulk.
7. Mix the combination until it forms a smoother puree, adding more water if needed.
8. Allow the puree to come to a boil.
9. Insert the cornflour mixture and whisk briefly.
10. To create corn flour powder, combine one tablespoon rice flour and ¼ cup water in a mixing bowl.
11. Check the quality by stirring once more.
12. Then, in a serving cup, drain the soup and finish with fresh milk.

8.4 Easy One-Pot Corn Soup

Cooking Time: 30 minutes
Serving Size: 6

Ingredients:
- 5 eggs large, beaten
- 1 teaspoon sesame oil
- 5 tablespoon green onions
- ¼ cup cornstarch
- 1 can corn
- 1 can creamed corn
- 1 tablespoon soy sauce
- 1 cup carrots
- 7 cups chicken broth
- Pepper to taste
- 1 tablespoon sriracha sauce
- 2.5 cups chicken
- 1-2 teaspoon ginger powder
- Salt to taste
- 1-2 teaspoon garlic powder

Method:
1. Take broth, grilled chicken, ginger, garlic, salt, spice, Sriracha sauce, sesame oil, vegetables, corn, cheesed corn, and two tablespoons of fresh basil boil over a moderate flame in a big nonstick pan.
2. Reduce the heat to medium-low and cook for another 8-10 minutes, just until the carrots are tender.
3. Mix with the diluted cornstarch slurry. The broth will thicken as it cooks.
4. Slowly pour in the beaten eggs, stirring gently to create fried egg ribbons.

5. Mix with the remaining three tablespoons, spring onions, and sesame oil.
6. Switch off the heat and serve right away.

8.5 Creamy Bottle Gourd Soup

Cooking Time: 20 minutes
Serving Size: 3

Ingredients:
- Salt and black pepper
- Cilantro
- 1 medium onion
- 1.5 cups water
- 1 medium bottle gourd
- 3 medium garlic cloves
- 1 green chili
- 1 teaspoon olive oil

Method:
1. In the Instant Pot, choose to sauté mode.
2. When the olive oil is sweet, add the minced garlic, vegetables, and green chilies and cook until the onions are softened.
3. Combine the diced bottle gourd, liquid or veggie broth, and salt in a large mixing bowl.
4. Set the timer for five minutes and the container to manual.
5. Allow the pressure to escape as the instant port buzzes spontaneously.
6. Then use a stand mixer, puree the soup until it is almost creamy.
7. Season with black pepper, ground.
8. If desired, garnish with cilantro just before eating.

8.6 Roasted Tomato Soup

Cooking Time: 50 minutes
Serving Size: 6

Ingredients:
- ½ cup basil leaves
- ¾ cup heavy cream
- 2 bay leaves
- 4 tablespoons butter
- 2 ½ pounds fresh tomatoes
- Salt and black pepper
- 1-quart chicken stock
- 6 cloves garlic
- Vine cherry tomatoes
- ½ cup extra-virgin olive oil
- 2 small yellow onions

Method:
1. Preheat the oven to 450 degrees Fahrenheit.
2. Tomatoes should be washed, cored, and sliced in half.
3. On a baking tray, arrange the tomatoes, peppercorns, and vegetables.
4. Sprinkle with salt and drizzle with ½ cup olive oil.
5. Switch the diced peppers, onion, and garlic to a big stockpot from the stove.
6. ¾ chicken stock, garlic cloves, and butter are added.
7. If using, wipe down basil leaves before adding them to the bowl.
8. Erase the bay leaves before pureeing the soup with an electric mixer until creamy.
9. Sprinkle with salt and ground black pepper to satisfy.

10. Three or four roasted grape sun-dried tomatoes and a dash of heavy cream can be garnished in the dish.

8.7 Carrot Tomato Soup

Cooking Time: 1 hour and 15 minutes
Serving Size: 8

Ingredients:
- 1 tablespoon red wine vinegar
- 250ml whole milk
- 2 vegetable stock cubes
- 1 tablespoon sugar
- 3 tablespoon olive oil
- 500g carton passata
- 750g cherry tomato
- 2 onions
- 250g floury potato
- 5 bay leaves
- 1¼ kg carrot
- 2 celery sticks

Method:
1. In your biggest frying pan, softly steam the oil, onion, and fennel until cooled.
2. For several minutes, add the potatoes and carrots, and add all of the rest of the ingredients, except the milk, along with 1-liter water.
3. Take to a low boil, then reduce to low heat.
4. Cover and cook for thirty minutes, then open and continue to cook for another thirty minutes.
5. Remove the basil leaves and mix the broth with a hand blender until smooth.

6. Pour in the milk or as much water as necessary.
7. Adjust with salt and pepper to taste, then warm through it and eat with the crispy hot cross buns.

8.8 Cream of Broccoli Soup

Cooking Time: 35 minutes
Serving Size: 6

Ingredients:
- 2 cups milk
- Ground black pepper
- 8 cups broccoli florets
- 3 tablespoons all-purpose flour
- 5 tablespoons butter
- 1 stalk celery
- 3 cups chicken broth
- 1 onion

Method:
1. A moderate, slow cooker, melt two tablespoons of butter and sauté tomato and fennel until soft.
2. Cover and cook for an additional with the broccoli and broth.
3. In a mixer, puree the broth. Blend in batches until light and fluffy, then transfer to a clean pot.
4. Peel 3 tablespoons butter in a small saucepan, then stir in flour and dairy.
5. Stir once thick, then bubbly, and transfer to the broth.
6. Serve with a pinch of black pepper.

Chapter 9: Indian Salad Recipes

9.1 Bean Sprouts and Salad Recipe

Cooking Time: 12 minutes
Serving Size: 2

Ingredients:
- 1 green onion
- 9 oz. bean sprouts

Seasonings
- ½ tablespoon soy sauce
- ¼ teaspoon kosher/sea salt
- 1 clove garlic
- 1 tablespoon sesame oil
- 1 tablespoon white sesame seeds

Method:
1. Dump the bean sprouts thoroughly after rinsing them in cold water.
2. A huge pot of water should be brought to a boil.
3. Once the water has come to a boil, add the bean sprouts and simmer for 2 - 5 minutes.
4. Drain and set it aside for five minutes in a saucepan.
5. Break the spring onions into small bits in the meantime.
6. In a pestle and mortar, ground the caraway seeds.
7. Grate or grind the garlic cloves with a garlic press.
8. Combine all of the spice components in a medium mixing bowl and stir well.
9. In a large mixing cup, add the bean sprouts and spring onions.

10. Freeze or serve at ambient temperature.

9.2 Broccoli and Baby Corn Salad

Cooking Time: 15 minutes
Serving Size: 6

Ingredients:

Salad Ingredients
- 1 large carrot grated
- ¼ cup cranberries
- 1 cup cherry tomatoes
- ½ can produce corn or corn
- 2 medium broccoli

Dressing Ingredients
- 4 tablespoon mayo
- 1 large garlic clove
- 4 tablespoon ranch

Method:
1. Broccoli should be chopped into small thin strips.
2. Merge sliced broccoli, two tablespoons sliced tomatoes, corn cobs, one red onion, and ¼ cup blueberries in a large mixing bowl.
3. Combine four tablespoon ranch dressing, four tablespoon mayonnaise, and 2 pressed garlic powder in a shallow mixing bowl or measuring cup.
4. Toss the salad with the dressing and adjust the seasonings to taste.

9.3 Rajma Salad

Cooking Time: 40 minutes

Serving Size: 4

Ingredients:
- Mint leaves
- Salt, to taste
- 1 teaspoon chaat masala powder
- 1 lemon, juiced
- 2 cups rajma
- 1 tomato
- 2 green chilies
- 1 onion

Method:
1. Soak the rajma overtime and pressure bake for four to six whistles with water.
2. Reduce the heat to low and continue to cook for the next 20 minutes after four to six whistles.
3. Enable the pressure to dissipate normally. Rajma must be roasted and soft.
4. Drain the accumulated water and set aside the rajma if there is any.
5. Add the chopped rajma, carrots, peppers, green chile sauce, chaat masala paste, salt, fresh mint, and lime juice to a mixing cup.
6. Toss the rajma salad together thoroughly.
7. Taste for salt and change as needed. Chill before serving.

9.4 Paneer and Chana Salad

Cooking Time: 30 minutes
Serving Size: 3

Ingredients:
- 1 tablespoon lime juice
- 1 teaspoon virgin olive oil

- 1 green chili
- Salt as required
- 1 cup soaked chickpeas
- ½ cup cubed paneer
- 1 tomato
- 4 leaves spinach
- 1 handful coriander leaves
- black pepper
- 1 onion
- ½ teaspoon chaat masala powder
- 1 handful black olives

Method:
1. To make this tasty salad, drench the chickpeas overnight and cook them until tender.
2. Slice the cabbage, green chilies, and onion in the meantime.
3. Merge the paneer balls, chickpeas, and sliced veggies in a big mixing cup.
4. Add the green olives and cut the basil leaf.
5. To make the dressing, whisk together the canola oil, chaat masala paste, lime juice, and spice powder in a mixing cup.
6. Toss the salad in this sauce thoroughly. Serve with cilantro as a garnish.

9.5 Healthy Lunch Salad

Cooking Time: 20 minutes
Serving Size: 6

Ingredients:
- 1 large ripe avocado
- ½ tablespoon mixed sesame seeds

- ½ cucumber
- 3 spring onions
- 250g sirloin steaks
- 12 radishes
- 3 carrots
- Thumb-sized piece ginger
- 3 red bird's eye chilies
- 4 lettuces
- 2 tablespoon sesame oil
- 1 tablespoon low-salt soy sauce
- 2 limes, juiced
- 1 garlic clove

Method:
1. Prepare the salad dressing by stirring together all the garlic, ginger, lemon zest, oil, oil, and minced chilies in a cup just before frying.
2. Place the steaks on the grill and bake for three minutes on the one hand, then change and grill for another three minutes for medium-rare.
3. Wrap and set aside the meat for five minutes after it has finished cooking.
4. On a shared tray, place the salad leaves, radishes, cabbage, grapefruit, green onions, and avocado.
5. Cut the steak thinly against the grains and serve on top of the lettuce.
6. Drizzle any remaining juices and seasoning over the top.
7. Serve with sesame oil and cut red chili as a garnish.

9.6 Bean Sprout and Macaroni Salad

Cooking Time: 30 minutes

Serving Size: 8

Ingredients:

Soy-Ginger Dressing
- 2 tablespoons mayonnaise
- ¼ cup vegetable oil
- 1 teaspoon ground ginger
- ¾ teaspoon pepper flakes
- 1 tablespoon sugar
- 1 tablespoon sesame oil
- 6 tablespoons soy sauce
- 1 tablespoon rice wine vinegar
- 3 medium garlic

Pasta Salad
- ½ cup peanuts
- ¼ cup cilantro
- 2 cups bean sprouts
- 3 green onions
- 3 medium carrots
- 1 medium red bell pepper
- 2 tablespoons salt
- 8 ounces broccoli florets
- 1 pound beef
- 1 pound penne pasta

Method:
1. In a 2-cup Pyrex mason jar, combine the garlic, sesame oil, salt, starch, soy sauce, spice, and pepper seasoning.
2. Mix in the tomato sauce until dry, then drizzle in the oil in a long, steady stream to create an emulsions dressing; chill until prepared to use.
3. In a big soup pot, bring 1 liter of water and two teaspoons of salt to a simmer.

4. Insert the spaghetti and cook until only tender, whisking frequently and incorporating the broccoli over the last moment.
5. Set aside as you finish cooking the rest of the salad ingredients.
6. Combine all salad ingredients in a big mixing bowl or a gallon-size zip pack.
7. When ready to eat, insert the dressing and toss it to cover.

9.7 Peas and Potato Salad

Cooking Time: 45 minutes
Serving Size: 6

Ingredients:
- ½ teaspoon salt
- ¼ cup red onion
- 1 tablespoon apple cider vinegar
- 1 teaspoon dried tarragon
- 2 lbs. red potatoes
- ¾ cup mayonnaise
- 1 tablespoon Dijon mustard
- ½ cup frozen peas

Method:
1. Get a pan of salted water to a boil with the potatoes.
2. Reduce heat to low and continue to cook until the vegetables are tender.
3. Add peas for two minutes until the potatoes are finished.
4. Drain the water and set it aside to cool to ambient temperature.
5. Potatoes can be cut into wedges.

6. Merge mayonnaise, vinegar, mustard, thyme, and salt in a big mixing cup.
7. Toss in the potatoes, beans, and sliced onion until it is evenly covered.
8. Refrigerate for 1 hour until it is ready to use.

9.8 Cabbage and Grape Salad

Cooking Time: 35 minutes
Serving Size: 4

Ingredients:
- ¼ cup sunflower seeds
- 2 tablespoons chives
- ½ small red cabbage
- 1½ cups seedless grapes
- 2 tablespoons red wine vinegar
- Kosher salt and pepper
- ¼ cup olive oil
- 1 teaspoon dijon mustard
- ½ teaspoon thyme
- ½ teaspoons sugar

Method:
1. In a big mixing cup, combine red wine vinegar, salt, cayenne pepper, minced chives, kosher salt, and a few squeezes of pepper.
2. Add the olive oil and whisk to combine.
3. Combine sliced red cabbage, doubled seedless grapes, pickled roasted seeds, and sliced chives in a shallow mixing bowl.
4. Season with salt and pepper.
5. Allow for at least a few minutes of resting time before serving.

Chapter 10: Most Famous Indian Dishes

10.1 Rajma Chawal

Cooking Time: 45 minutes
Serving Size: 4

Ingredients:
- 1 tablespoon black pepper
- 1 tablespoon ghee
- 1 tablespoon garam masala powder
- 1 black cardamom
- 1 cup red kidney beans
- 1 tablespoon cumin powder
- Salt as required
- 1 tablespoon garlic
- 2 chopped green chili
- 2 large tomato
- 1 cup rice
- 2 clove
- 3 tablespoon mustard oil
- 2 large onion
- 1 cinnamon stick
- 2 green cardamom
- 1 teaspoon ginger
- 1 tablespoon black pepper
- 1 tablespoon coriander powder

Method:
1. Rajma should be washed.

2. Pressure cook with 2 cups sugar, one tablespoon salt, and turmeric.
3. Finely cut the onions and set them aside, as well as the tomatoes, which should be grated and set aside.
4. Get a spice, onion, and sweet chili paste.
5. Add mustard oil to a depth skillet.
6. Cook until lightly browned, then add the onions.
7. Heat on medium for 4-5 minutes after adding the tomatoes.
8. Combine the ginger, cloves, and sweet chili sauce, as well as the spices.
9. Cook until the spices are fragrant and the oil begins to run down the sides of the pan.
10. Now insert one cup of hot water and the rajma.
11. Pour the rice into the water.
12. Strain the water until the rice is soft and doubled in size.
13. Enable the rice to cool for 2-3 minutes after spreading it out on a pan.
14. Serve immediately with the Rajma that has been prepared.

10.2 Lucknowi Biryani

Cooking Time: 40 minutes
Serving Size: 6

Ingredients:
- 1 pinch saffron
- 1 large onion
- 3 teaspoon ghee
- 4 tablespoon refined oil
- ½ teaspoon mace powder
- 2 black cardamom

- 1 inches cinnamon stick
- 1 teaspoon fennel seeds
- 1 teaspoon black pepper
- 2 cup basmati rice
- 10 clove
- 2 teaspoon cumin seeds
- 2 teaspoon salt
- 2½ cup milk
- 2 teaspoon coriander seeds
- 3 green cardamom
- ½ kilograms mutton
- 2-star anise

For Marination
- 1 teaspoon red chili powder
- 1 pinch garam masala powder
- 4 teaspoon yogurt
- 1 teaspoon garlic paste
- 1 teaspoon ginger paste
- 2 teaspoon cashews
- 1 teaspoon turmeric

Method:
1. Dry roast all of the whole ingredients to make garam masala. Fold the quantity of water used to boil the rice.
2. Combine the food items for meat marination. Refrigerate it for an hour after covering it with a plate.
3. Finely chop the onion and cook it in a little oil before setting it aside. Salt and pepper the beef. In the handi, combine the peanut oil and the oil. Switch the marinated steak from the container to the handi until it is hot enough.

4. On high heat, stir and simmer the meat for a few seconds. In the meantime, transfer the saffron to the dairy and stir well to unleash the saffron color and scent into the milk. The mutton can now be layered with cooked rice, followed by the saffron cooking liquid.
5. Cover your handiwork. Cook for about 30 minutes and serve.

10.3 Chana Masala

Cooking Time: 35 minutes
Serving Size: 4

Ingredients:
- Lemon wedges
- Fresh cilantro
- 1 large can of tomatoes
- 2 cans chickpeas
- 1 cup basmati rice
- ½ teaspoon turmeric
- Pinch of cayenne pepper
- 2 tablespoons coconut oil
- 1 ½ teaspoons coriander
- ¾ teaspoon cumin
- 1 onion
- 1 tablespoon ginger
- 1 ½ teaspoons garam masala
- ½ teaspoon fine sea salt
- 5 cloves garlic
- 1 serrano

Method:
1. Prepare the rice. Remove the cap and fluff the grain with a spoon, seasoning to taste with kosher salt.
2. Add the oil in a small Dutch oven or big saucepan over medium-low heat.
3. Combine the carrot, chiles, and salt in a mixing bowl.
4. Cook for about five minutes or until the onions are soft.
5. Cook for 30 seconds to 1 minute, till the cloves and spice are fragrant.
6. Cook, stirring continuously, for the next minute after adding the spices.
7. Toss in the tomatoes, along with their juices.
8. Add the lentils and boost the oven temperature.
9. Take the combination to a low boil, then reduce to low heat.
10. If needed, season with more salt to taste.
11. If chosen, pour-over basmati rice with a lemon slice or two and a sprinkling of dried basil leaves.

10.4 Kadhi Chawal

Cooking Time: 55 minutes
Serving Size: 5

Ingredients:
For Kadhi
- 1 chili
- 2 tablespoon coriander
- Pinch asafoetida
- 1 onion
- One teaspoon coriander seeds
- 1 dried red chili

- 1 teaspoon jeera
- ½ teaspoon pepper
- 5 tablespoon gram flour
- 2 tablespoon oil
- ½ teaspoon fenugreek
- 1 cup yogurt
- 5 cup water
- ½ teaspoon turmeric
- ½ tablespoon ginger garlic paste
- 1 teaspoon salt
- ¼ teaspoon carom seeds
- 1 teaspoon red chili powder

For Tempering
- 1 dried red chili
- ½ teaspoon red chili powder
- 1 teaspoon cumin
- 1 tablespoon ghee

Method:
1. First, combine the besan, turmeric, chili powder, ajwain, spice garlic paste, pepper, and curd in a large mixing bowl.
2. Mix thoroughly to create a stable paste.
3. Now add 4 cups of water and stir thoroughly. Set aside for now.
4. Two tablespoons oil, ½ teaspoon methi, one teaspoon smoked paprika, ½ teaspoon salt, one teaspoon cilantro seeds, one red chili, and pinch hing heated in a wide wok.
5. Prepare the pakoras according to the package directions.
6. Pour the pakoras into the kadhi that has been packed.
7. Heat 1 tablespoon ghee to make the tempering.

8. Add two tablespoons coriander to the tempering and spill over the kadhi. Blend well.
9. Finally, serve the kadhi pakora with boiled vegetables or jeera rice.

10.5 Masala Dosa

Cooking Time: 1 hour
Serving Size: 10

Ingredients:
For the Dosa Batter
- ½ teaspoon salt
- Vegetable oil
- One teaspoon fenugreek seeds
- ½ cup urad dal
- 2 cups short-grain rice

For the Potato Filling
- 1 ½ pounds potatoes
- ½ cup cilantro
- 4 garlic cloves, minced
- 2 small green chiles
- 1 tablespoon grated ginger
- 8 curry leaves
- 3 tablespoons ghee
- ½ teaspoon turmeric
- Pinch of asafetida
- 1 teaspoon mustard seeds
- 1 medium onion
- ½ teaspoon salt
- 2 small hot red peppers
- ½ teaspoon cumin seeds

Method:

1. In a pan, clean the rice thoroughly and coat it with 4 cups of ice water.
2. In a small container, combine the urad dal and fenugreek nuts, rinse properly, and cover cold water.
3. In different colanders, drain the rice and the dal-fenugreek combination.
4. Fill a stick blender, mixer, or wet-dry slicer halfway with rice.
5. In a large mixing dish, combine two blends.
6. Add enough water to make a medium-thick mixture by whisking it together.
7. There should be around 6 cups total.
8. In a large skillet, melt ghee over medium-high heat.
9. Toss in the potatoes and half a cup of water.
10. Heat, constantly stirring, for around five minutes, or until the fluid has faded away.
11. Set a broiler pan or cast-iron pan over medium heat to create dosas.
12. ½ teaspoon oil drizzled over the edge.
13. Allow dosa batter to color on one side only until the outer layers start to look clean, about two minutes.
14. Marginally deflate the potato blend. Cook and serve right away.

10.6 Dal Makhani

Cooking Time: 2 hours 10 minutes
Serving Size: 5

Ingredients:
To Pressure Cook
- 1 teaspoon salt
- 3.5 cups water

- ¼ cup rajma
- ¾ cup urad dal

Masala for the Dal
- More Amul butter
- Piece of charcoal
- ½ teaspoon sugar
- ¼ cup cream
- 1 tablespoon ghee
- ½ teaspoon salt or to taste
- 1.5 cups water
- 3 tablespoons butter
- ½ teaspoon red chili powder
- ¼ teaspoon garam masala
- Two teaspoons ginger garlic
- ½ cup tomato puree
- 1 medium white onion

Method:
1. In a big mixing cup, rinse and wash the urad grain and rajma.
2. Add one teaspoon salt to the dal and rajma in a slow cooker.
3. Heat for ten minutes at medium temperature, then reduce to the low-medium pan and stir for another ten minutes.
4. Then use a stick blender, mix some of the dal and rajma.
5. Warm two tablespoons of oil in a pan, in order to make the paratha.
6. Heat for 1 to 2 minutes after adding the spice garlic paste.

7. Toss in the tomato puree and blend well.
8. Add in the dal that has been boiled.
9. Curry paste, red chili paste, and salt are added to the pan.
10. Stir in ½ cup water and reduce heat to low.
11. Just after dal has stewed for 45 minutes, add the butter and blend well.
12. Position the steel bowl on the tops of the trivet and fill it with hot charcoal.
13. Ghee should be heated and poured on top of the charcoal.
14. Represent with a tap of Amul oil and more milk on top of the dal makhani.

10.7 Rogan Josh

Cooking Time: 2 hours 20 minutes
Serving Size: 5

Ingredients:
- 1 ½ tablespoon fennel powder
- 1 ¼ tablespoon flour
- 2 pinch saffron
- 1 tablespoon red chili powder
- 1 kilograms mutton
- 4 red chili
- 1 ¼ tablespoon coriander powder
- ½ teaspoon asafoetida
- 1 ¼ teaspoon cumin seeds
- 1 teaspoon peppercorns
- 2 cinnamon

- 2 ½ tablespoon milk
- 150 gm hung curd
- 5 black cardamom
- Salt as required
- ½ cup ghee
- One ¼ teaspoon ginger powder
- 1 ½ cup water

For Garnishing
- Coriander leaves

Method:
1. To make this delicious taste, first, make the saffron dairy by boiling saffron in milk for several hours.
2. Then, in the slow cooker, add entire red chilies, chopped garlic, and asafetida and cook for few seconds.
3. After that, add the meat bits and stir thoroughly.
4. Remove the cap after 5 minutes and add ½ cup of water, stirring well with the seasoning.
5. In the meantime, in a shallow mixing cup, combine all-purpose flour and yogurt, and stir well.
6. In a large mixing bowl, combine all of the spices.
7. Later, in the slow cooker, add 1 cup of water and steam the meat for 1-2 hours on medium.
8. Marinade and serve immediately with chapati or hummus.
9. This recipe can also be served with rice.

Conclusion

India's culinary is one of the most versatile in the world, distinguished by its refined and delicate use of the many herbs, spices, seeds, and fruits produced throughout the country. The diverse populations of the culturally mixed Indian subcontinent are reflected in each geographical region's culinary, including a wide variety of recipes and prepared foods. The spiritual traditions and culture of India have influenced the development of its food. Many Buddhist, Hindu, and Jain cultures follow a vegetarian diet. For its long cultural impact on the continent's food cultures, Indian cuisine is common in Southeast Asia. The middle ages saw the impact of Indian cuisine on traditional Malaysian recipes. Vegetarianism's spread across Asia is mostly attributed to old Hindu Buddhist traditions. When it comes to various spices in Indian cuisine, there are many health benefits. Prepare foods, explore with ingredients, and use these dishes to enjoy a healthier and more enjoyable life.

Printed in Great Britain
by Amazon